When People
Do You Wrong

by

Horace L. Patterson, Sr.

D0967376

MEGA
CORPORATION

Nashville, Tennessee

When People
Do You Wrong

by
Horace L. Patterson Sr.

MEGA
CORPORATION

Copyright © 2001
MEGA Corporation
Nashville, Tennessee

ISBN: 1-890436-22-4
Printed in the United States of America

In tribute to
Ida and Will Patterson,
Mother and Father,
and
Dolia and George McIntosh,
Mother-in-law and Father-in-law,
who now live with God.

• About the Author •

Dr. Horace L. Patterson, Sr. has received the World Leadership Award and the Certificate of Merit from the International Biographical Center located in Cambridge, England. The author holds several degrees from Alabama colleges, including Bachelor of Theology and Doctor of Divinity degrees from Selma University, a B.A. in clinical psychology from Talladega College, and an M.S. in counseling from Jacksonville State University.

For ten years Dr. Patterson served as a member of the Talladega City Board of Education, was elected to the Talladega City Council for three consecutive terms, and is the originator of fulfillment counseling (a Christian insight-oriented approach to counseling). Having worked as a psychotherapist, program supervisor, and division director in the clinical mental health arena, he employs a wide range of professional mastery.

The author has served as pastor of churches in Michigan and throughout Alabama. Currently, he is senior pastor of the historic Mount Canaan Baptist Church in Talladega, where he has served for more than 25 years, and is the state-wide coordinator for senior services for the Alabama Institute for the Deaf and Blind.

• Contents •

- Introduction -

Being wronged is never easy. We can accept painful changes in circumstances outside of human control. We can even accept discomforts caused by people, as long as we perceive their actions as unintentional . But when people purposefully wrong us and appear indifferent and remorseless, we are confronted with a test from a different page of life.

When struck, we want to strike back. It is innate. it is normal. it is human. When hurt, we want to hurt back. If we can see a person cringe the way we did; well, that's another story. We are products of a society whose cry is "fight fire with fire" and "do unto others before they get a chance to do unto you." When the Berlin Wall and the Soviet Union were dismantled, our national belief system that "might is right" was reinforced rather than challenged.

We do not simply have divorces, we have "messy divorces." We have eleven-year-old hit-men, and children — ten and eleven years old — throwing a five year old out of a fourteen-story apartment building because he would not steal for them. We have focused on making the world "safe for democracy," but in reality, our most formidable enemies live inside our own city limits.

People hurt people, and when pain is repaid with pain, nobody wins. Society suffers. Dangerous lessons are taught, and deadly lessons are learned. In Union, South Carolina, a mother admits to drowning her own sons. Prior to her admission, she had described an African-American male who carjacked her car and kidnapped her children. A manhunt for a fictitious character ensued. Upon her admission of guilt, many African-Americans were outraged because unfounded, stereotypical labeling placed African-Americans in the middle of the situation. There was a feeling of being mistreated again simply because old ideas are not easily discarded. Old wounds left their scars, and the theme of pain reasserted its sting. We need many things, but there is nothing that we need more than the ability to overcome our libelous wounds and move on with our lives in a productive manner. We *can* rise from the dust. We can grow wiser instead of weary, and we can experience "spiritual deepening" rather than harmful hostility.

Historically, we speak of "the shot heard around the world," which started the American Revolution, and I am convinced that future generations will speak of an explosion that was felt around the world on April 19, 1995. On that Wednesday morning, the thousand-pound bomb that ripped the heart out of a federal office building in Oklahoma City, Oklahoma, did unmeasured damage to us all. Innocent children learning their ABC's in a daycare center, senior citizens signing up for their well-deserved social security, and civil servants in their daily routine — all fell prey to a madness that shook most of us in ways we had never known.

In response to that madness, we are caught between a search for justice and a desire for revenge. In theory, we know that revenge is not the answer, but in reality, we are put to a test that is far more complicated than any of us could have anticipated prior to such devastation. However, revenge must be overruled by the response of a caring nation. Justice, yes — revenge, no. Justice, yes — because the blood of the innocent cries from the massive mixture of cable and concrete. Revenge, no — because their lives and their sacrificial departure should affect us in deeper ways. Justice, yes — because they must know from the world beyond this world that their lives mattered, and that they are missed. Revenge, no — because their memories must not be stained with anything that is less than a noble quest and an honorable end. Justice, yes — because it is right. Revenge, no — because it is wrong. Justice, yes — because evil must be dealt with. Revenge, no — because we must never become partners with the force that we are fighting.

While individually we do not often experience being wronged at the dramatic level that we have known as a result of the "Terror in the Heartland," we do each see and sense our own personal and tailored attacks. We are called not simply to endure, but to profit from our trials. Our circumstances become truly effectual when they elicit unique changes in our lives. Our pains, too, can be catalysts for positive effects as we allow them to change us into better people. The death of loved ones ought to make us more appreciative of life. The things that matter ought not be confused with the things that matter most. A job matters, but the person on the job matters more. A slamming door matters, but the person who slammed the door matters more. A stain on the carpet matters, but the child who stained the carpet matters more. The mate who keeps us waiting is always more important than the time we lost waiting. What matters is not always what matters most.

In this book, you will be challenged to appreciate the ministry of pain and the wisdom it produces. You will laugh. You might even cry. But as you make this journey, you will surely grow. My prayer and hope is that you will deal with the things that matter but never confuse them with the things that matter most.

- ONE -

FACING THE FACTS

A wrong committed against us is like a blazing fire. We can feed it, or we can extinguish it. We can give it a house to live in that it will eventually burn down, or we can overcome it and move on with our lives in a much wiser manner. I am an advocate of the latter because the alternative is far too costly.

A father lashes out at his innocent children because his work day went poorly. After hearing that her boyfriend called another girl, the crazed teenager goes after him with a single-edge razor. A spouse discovers infidelity in a mate and, instead of addressing the issues, lets them smolder within until they become a raging inferno. A gun is discovered in a student's book bag at school because of an insult the previous day. Such acts remind us that we can make ourselves into greater victims, instead of working in productive ways to receive the very things, that we say we desperately want. If we don't handle the wrongs committed against us, they will handle us in ways that will continue to fill our cemeteries and break our hearts.

The handwritten diary filled with German words, Nazi rhetoric, and messages of hate reveals that the two gunmen responsible for the massacre at Columbine High School had been plotting their lethal rampage for almost a year. The diary, found in the home of one of the gunmen, contains a detailed timeline of events beginning in April, 1998. A final entry on the day of the Tuesday attack declared, "It's time to rock and roll," or words to that effect, according to law enforcement officials. The diary reveals that the killers picked a time when the largest numbers of students would be in the school cafeteria, that they planned to burn the school down, and that the massacre was intentionally timed to coincide with Adolf Hitler's birth date, April 20. It also reveals that the killers expected to die in the massacre.

In that bloody assault, Eric Hanson, eighteen, and Dylan Klebold, seventeen, attacked their classmates with sawed-off shotguns, semi-automatic weapons, and pipe bombs, killing twelve students and a teacher. They also scattered more than thirty bombs and booby traps in the building, including a hidden thirty-five pound bomb made with a propane tank. "If you are reading this, my mission is complete," one message says. "Your children who have ridiculed me, who have chosen not to accept me, who have treated me like I am not worth their time, are dead." Near the end, it warns that "more extensive death is to come" and finishes: "You have until April 26th. Goodbye."

February 2, 1996: A fourteen-year-old boy wearing a trench coat walks into algebra class with a hunting rifle and allegedly opens fire, killing the teacher and two students. A third student is injured during the shooting at a junior high school in Moses Lake, Washington.

February 19, 1997: A sixteen-year-old student opens fire with a shotgun in a common area at the Bethel, Alaska, high school, killing the principal and a student. Two other students are wounded. Authorities later accuse two other students of knowing the shootings would take place. Evan Ramsey was sentenced to two ninety-nine-year terms.

October 1, 1997: A sixteen-year-old outcast in Pearl, Mississippi, is accused of killing his mother, then going to Pearl High School and shooting nine students. Two of them die, including the suspect's ex-girlfriend. The sixteen year old is sentenced to life in prison. Two others await trial on accessory charges.

December 1, 1997: Three students are killed and five others wounded while they take part in a prayer circle in a hallway at Heath High School in West Paducah, Kentucky. A fourteen year old student pleads guilty, but mentally ill, to murder and is serving life in prison. One of the wounded girls is left paralyzed.

March 24, 1998: Four girls and a teacher are shot to death, and ten others wounded during a false fire alarm at Westside Middle School in Jonesboro, Arkansas, when two boys, aged eleven and thirteen, open fire from nearby woods. Both are convicted in juvenile court of murder and can be held until age twenty-one.

April 24, 1998: A forty-eight year old science teacher is shot to death in front of students at a graduation dance in Edinboro, Pennsylvania. A fourteen year old student at James W. Parker Middle School is charged.

April 28, 1998: Two teenage boys are shot to death and a third is wounded as they play basketball at a Pomona, California, elementary school hours after classes had ended. A fourteen year old boy is charged; the shooting is blamed on rivalry between two groups of youths.

May 19, 1998: Three days before his graduation, an eighteen year old honor student allegedly opens fire in a parking lot at Lincoln County High School in Fayetteville, Tennessee, killing a classmate who was dating his ex-girlfriend.

May 21, 1998: Three sixth-grade boys have a "hit list" and are plotting to kill fellow classmates on the last day of school in a sniper attack during a false fire alarm, according to police in St. Charles, Missouri.

May 21, 1998: A fifteen year old student in Springfield, Oregon, expelled the day before for bringing a gun to school, allegedly opens fire in the school cafeteria. Two students are killed. The suspect's parents are later found shot dead in their home.

April 20, 1999: Two young men wearing long, black trench coats opened fire in a suburban high school in Littleton, Colorado, injuring as many as twenty students. In all, fifteen were killed, including the two gunmen.

"Whom the gods would destroy they first make mad" — an ancient proverb that our society could use to great benefit. The Holy Bible says in Proverbs 27:4 that, "Wrath is cruel, and anger is outrageous; but who is able to stand before envy?" The Bible goes on to provide an answer in Psalm 76:10, "The wrath of man shall praise thee." God is eternally able to make the wrath of men praise Him, if we cooperate. I once heard a story about a minister who was leading a religious service. A drunken man threw a well-aimed potato, which found its mark on the minister's face. The minister was momentarily sidetracked but regained his composure and finished the service. After the service concluded, the minister prayed with the potato in hand, and a voice seemed to say, "Plant it!" The minister obeyed. A whole basket of potatoes was harvested from a potato thrown with unkind motives. We are often the recipients of many wrongs thrown at us. When people, in their wrath, hurl cruel wrongs at us, they may also be sowing seeds that will bear a mighty harvest.

Education or Enslavement

Three men are my friends.
He who hates me, he who loves me,
And he who is indifferent to me.
He who hates me teaches me caution;
He who loves me teaches me tenderness;
He who is indifferent to me teaches me self-reliance.
Three men are my friends!

— Author Unknown

This writer made the decision to be educated rather than enslaved, regardless of the unwanted actions of others. You can hinder a person like that, but you can't stop a person with that outlook. That kind of person never quits even when they are knocked down. Strong faith in God can make the future our friend. Our attitudes often determine the effects of being wronged.

Hiding the truth will not change it any more than ignoring the truth will nullify it. The truth is, being wronged by another person is the price we pay for social interaction. It is not simply the cost we expend for human relations but the price extracted as a result of having human contact. Being wronged is a risk we take that runs from the dishonest cab driver to the hurtful lover or family member. As we enter the twenty-first century, we also are faced with the premature end of far too many lives.

The Gunslinger Mentality

In spite of technological advancements, we have regressed to the mindset of the old west. We have become a nation of deadly streets. In far too many ways we are enslaved by violence. The National Center for Health Statistics points out that everyday, fourteen children, under the age of nineteen, are killed by bullets. The FBI Uniform Crime Report recently revealed a year when more than 24,000 people were killed by bullets in the United States.

The prophet Ezekiel spoke in his day to a suffering people and said, "The land devourest up men, and hast bereaved thy nation" (Ezek. 36:13). When compared to other nations during the twentieth century, the facts resound a tragic and urgent call for us to put out those fires. Firearm homicide is the leading cause of death for black males aged ten to thirty-four (National Center for Health Statistics). In 1990, handguns were used to murder ten people in Australia, thirteen in Sweden, twenty-two in Great Britain, sixty-eight in Canada, eighty-seven in Japan, ninety-one in Switzerland, and 10,567 in the United States (Embassies and foreign crime reporting agencies, FBI Uniform Crime Reports). Every day, an estimated 100,000 American students bring guns to school (National Education Association). There are more than one million illegal guns in New York City, and half of them belong to children (Bureau of Alcohol, Tobacco, and Firearms). In 1990, nearly three of four juvenile murder offenders used guns to perpetrate their crimes (FBI Uniform Crime Reports). The land is devouring men, women, and children. We are not handling matters, matters are handling us. Many disputes over simple, insignificant matters have been settled funeral services and at newly made graves.

Turning on the Light

We cannot isolate ourselves from the evil about us, but we can insulate ourselves against the evil that is around us. Meekness is strength under control, a far greater force than power out of control. The meek person is one who is strong enough to allow himself to be taught valuable lessons about self-reliance and caution, even from people who are indifferent and hateful.

He who hates me teaches me caution —
He who loves me teaches me tenderness —
He who is indifferent to me teaches me self-reliance.

None of us can determine what will happen in our lives, but we can always decide how those events will affect us. In every heartache there are some deep lessons to be learned. The hate of others need not weaken us. When properly managed, it can make us into stronger people. Unfriendly and unsympathetic critics often motivate us to present our best work because we know that they will make no excuses for mediocrity and seek to bring negative attention even when we are at our best. A member of my parish, Dr. T.Y. Lawrence, who now lives with God, was often quoted by his education students as saying, "Have an enemy read your term paper before I do, and your mistakes will be pointed out before you get to me!"

The person who hates you teaches you to check and recheck. He or she will drive you to dot those i's and cross those t's, and sometimes that hatred coming at you has a way of knocking the t off can't. When we are encircled by those who love us, we become careless. We take risks and make ambiguous statements that could be used to get us into a lot of trouble.

In the Book of 1 Samuel 18:5, the Bible says that David "behaved himself wisely" in the king's palace. Saul, the king, grew jealous. He threw a javelin, but David "avoided out of his presence twice" (18:11). Saul's persecution of David actually exposed David's greatness. The hottest fires produce the most flawless silver. God wants you to be patient because patience is the key that opens all of His other gifts. The wrongs committed by people who hate you can make you a better person, if you are cautious enough to avoid giving them the opportunity to misrepresent you. If your accusers get no help from you, the credibility of the charges will eventually be nullified. When people seek to persecute others, they work hard to vilify, the persecuted to those who might challenge or condemn their cruel behavior. Hitler first misrepresented Jews before he created the death camps. Hated people become objects of persecution, for their persecution is condoned as a justifiable consequence for the unknown deed that spawned the initial hatred. Native Americans were pictured savages. African-Americans were marketed as inferior to justify the evils done to them. Sometimes our greatest flaw is that we are not cautious enough. When people do you wrong, use their wrong-doings to make you a more cautious person. Caution will prevent many of your problems. Choose your battles. Pray for the right strategy. Understand that patience is not only a virtue, it is also a great spiritual weapon. The Psalmist says in Psalm 57:1, "Be merciful unto me, O God, be merciful unto me: for my soul trusteth in thee: yea, in the shadow of thy wings will I make my refuge, until these calamities be overpast."

It Will Pass

An Eastern ruler who had his share of troubles called for his wise men. They were given the assignment of coining a phrase that would help him in his hours of harassment. The phrase had to be brief enough to be engraved on a ring, yet it had to be relevant to every situation. After much thought and debate, they presented the ruler with these magnificent words. "This, too, shall pass away." In spite of afflictions we can find comfort, and in spite of our worries we can find hope, for no matter what it is that pains and confronts us, the fact is, "This, too, shall pass away."

Appreciation and Protection

The person who hates you also can teach you to appreciate the people who really love you. A sobering thought is that nobody has to love you. If one person can find the justification to hate you, so could the very person or people who love you dearly. There are no courts to mandate it and there are certainly no instruments available to enforce it. If we allow it, the cruelty of some people toward us can create in us a greater appreciation for those whose love we sometimes take for granted.

Growing or Swelling

There is a line in Shakespeare's Julius Caesar which says, "Some men grow, others swell. The fault, dear Brutus, is not in our stars but in ourselves." Dr. Viktor E. Frankl, the originator of logotherapy, spent three years at Auschwitz and other Nazi prison camps. He suffered many horrors during the Hitler regime. He reported that one of the first things that happened to incoming prisoners was that they were stripped naked. They were then looked upon and ridiculed. Some were raped, and all were treated subhuman. Dr. Frankl said he decided that no matter what they did to him or took from him, he would always react as a human being. I think that Shakespeare was right. "Some men grow, others swell. The fault, dear Brutus, is not in our stars but in ourselves."

We can choose to see problems in spite of possibilities or we can choose to see possibilities in spite of problems. An ancient cloth merchant entered a new land. He sent two representatives out to explore the market. One went north and the other went south. The man who went north wrote back saying, "The situation here is hopeless. we have no potential. None of the people here wear clothing." The agent who went south wrote back, enthusiastically, saying, "The situation here is very promising. We have an unlimited market. None of the people here wear clothing." One saw problems. One saw possibilities. The fault was not in the stars; it was in the person. You will be judged by what you finish, not by what you start. Life is a struggle. Pain in inevitable, but misery is a choice. We all have counterparts. One person goes through a divorce and sees it as the end of happiness — another person goes through a divorce and views it as the beginning of a chance to be happy. Some of the things that hurt us will eventually help us, but the things that really help us will not hurt us in the end. How we see what we see can spell the difference between growing in wisdom or swelling in anger and self-pity.

– Two –

Taught, But Not Controlled

Being taught by someone is not the same as being controlled by someone. If you let people who don't love you control you, they will sooner or later destroy you.

Insults

We make words very powerful when we let them elicit unhealthy responses from us. If a person who doesn't care for you can knowingly upset you by the use of words, that person has too much power over you. You've become a puppet controlled by the strings of their words. In the theories of behavior modification, there is a principle called reinforcement. An act takes place and the response to that act can reinforce or extinguish it. Your response tells people what works on you. Only when you let the offender know that the offense can control you emotionally do you almost guarantee that the strings will be pulled again. When you are wronged by an insult that you can live with, ignore it. If it is something that you choose not to endure and can create problems for the offender (for example, racial slurs, offensive sexual remarks), respond at a rational, intellectual level rather than an emotional level and mean it.

There Are No Exceptions

While degree and intent will vary, the reality of getting hurt is both universally experienced and uniquely appraised. Talent always outshines position. Lasting respect depends on the impact we make upon others. No person can claim or steal respect, but you can earn it. In a time of great stress and persecution, a missionary heard a rapid knock on his door. Some Christian people suffering intense persecution had come to him seeking his guidance. They pleaded with him for instructions saying, "Just tell us what to do! Just tell us what to do!" He listened attentively. He held his peace for a while. And then he spoke to them with the honesty that had characterized his life.

He said, "I cannot tell you what to do, but I can tell you who you are. He shared with them the "Peace of God which surpasseth human understanding" (Phil. 4:67), kissing their spirit, and they left rejoicing.

Don't Trust All That You Hear
And Be Wary of What You Don't Hear.

It was one hot, boring, summer day when those heat monkeys danced even on dirt roads. The sun dared you to look up, and all clothing seemed to stick to the skin like plastic glue before it hardens. I was young and didn't want to be. I had it made and didn't know it. Our neighbors had a lot of chickens, a chopping block, and a sharp ax. Red Bone and Mickey were playing with a chicken's life. Red Bone would hold the chicken's neck on the chopping block and snatch it away to prove that he could move fast enough to keep Mickey from chopping off the chicken's head. Red Bone lost! One dying chicken bounced around the yard until it realized that it was headless and died. To avoid trouble, they disposed of the chicken by throwing it in a well. I said they were neighbors. I didn't say they were smart. Their mother soon found out what they had done. She dealt with them by giving them a whipping. Mickey went in first. He took his whipping quietly. He didn't yell, he dried his eyes and walked back into the yard.

Red Bone: "What happened?"

Mickey: "Nothing."

Red Bone: "What do you mean, nothing?"

Mickey: "I mean nothing happened."

Red Bone: "Did you get a whipping?"

Mickey: "No way!"

Red Bone: "How did you do that?"

Mickey: "I just looked at her and I said, 'Woman don't you put your hands on me.' And she let me go."

Red Bone: "Well, if you didn't take it, I know I ain't gonna take it either."

A few minutes later, she called for Red Bone. He went into the house. There was a period of silence, then there were the rhythmic sounds and pain-racked woes of, "Oh, Lord! Mama, I didn't mean it," and "Mama, please don't kill me." Red Bone's lesson was quickly learned. You can't believe everything you hear, and you can't always trust the silence that you do hear. While Mickey had dried his eyes and muffled his cries, he had not been exempted. Red Bone had only his punishment increased by buying into an approach that defied common sense.

Don't Raise the Punishment Quotient

You can't come back from where you've never been. You can't push a rope. You can't make chicken salad out of chicken feathers, and you can't escape the fact that people hurt other people. Motives and intent differ, but the fact is universal. The only person unhurt by another is one who hasn't spend time with another. It is not unique to be hurt. What would be unique would be to live a useful life in a world like ours without ever getting hurt. However, the price for that might be the cost of our humanity. Remember, "It takes a whole lot of human feelings to be a human being."

No matter how often we are confronted with hurt, there is in each incident a kind of freshly made emotional incision. The good news is that we can determine how deep the cut goes. Unhealthy emotional reactions to a wrong committed against us can escalate to a physical liability. An argument can become a splitting headache. A false accusation can become a nagging ulcer. A shocking discovery can become a chest pain. *We get mad*, and *we make ourselves sick.* We try to get even, and we make ourselves sick. We try to get even, and we make ourselves ruthless. Ruthless people are not impossible to love in a godly manner, but they are hard to keep loving in a human way.

Not A Product — A Process

We are not a finished product, but as long as we are alive, we are involved in a process. A young girl was born with a disfigured face. She was loved deeply and surrounded by a very protective family. When it was time for her to go to school, she soon discovered how cruel other children could be. They made fun of her. She greeted her mother one evening and burst into tears. With the sincerity that only comes from a child, she looked up at her mother and asked, "Mother, why did God make me like this?" The mother answered her child with wisdom that is not born of this world. She said to her daughter as she pressed her to her bosom, "Honey, God is not through making you."

God is not finished making any of us. What seems to be a disaster today can become an open door tomorrow. The process is ongoing. The master potter not only bakes his vessels in the fire, he also floods them in the waters to make them both instruments of usefulness and objects of beauty. Pain by itself is evil, but pain viewed as a part of the process is redemptive. What you see is not all there is to see.

There is a thought-provoking story of a man who was admitted into paradise on the condition that he would not indulge in his old habit of criticism. In heaven he saw two angels carrying a beam crossways. They knocked the beam against every object they met. the man looked with strained eyes but said nothing. He looked again and this time, he saw two different angels drawing water from a fountain, then pouring the water into a barrel which had holes in the bottom. The man desperately wanted to say something, but he held his peace. Many other similar matters were noticed, but he suppressed his remarks fearing that he might suffer expulsion. Finally, the man saw a sight that broke his silence. A cart was stuck in the mud. One pair of horses was yoked to the front and another pair was yoked to the rear. The driver urged both pairs simultaneously forward.

The critic could not take it. He started to level out rebuking verbalizations. Suddenly, without speaking, two angels seized him and took him to the gate. However, before the gate closed behind him he looked back. To his amazement the horses had wings. They were pulling the cart from the mud into the air. What he thought made no sense put the cart into the clouds. The same cart that he thought should have been rolled was the one the driver knew should have been rising. The man saw horses pulling against each other. The driver saw horses ready to spread their wings. What the man thought he saw as a mistake, the driver knew as the right step to take to get out of the mud.

There are many ways to be stuck in the mud, and God has many ways to get us out. Sometimes we are moving in the right direction even when we feel like we are standing still. When people wrong us, it is not only God's will that we survive, it is sometimes his mandate that we soar as a result of it. Charles F. Kettering once said, "We should all be concerned about the future because we will have to spend the rest of our lives there."

Getting Even Is a Sisyphean Task

A Sisyphean task is one that is endless, difficult, and meaningless. The phrase is taken from a Greek mythological figure. In *The Odyssey*, Homer told a story of Sisyphus living in hell with the punishment of working long hours at a meaningless job.

He was cursed with the eternal torment of having to push an enormous boulder up a hill, only to have it roll back down just as he approached the crest. He would return to the bottom of the hill and begin his task again—all of this in a never-ending cycle.

Trying to get even with someone who has wronged you is as pointless a task as spending eternity rolling a huge stone up a hill only to have it roll back down. There was no real benefit in rolling the stone up the hill. The challenge of this difficult task so consumed Sisyphus that he did not give serious thought to the purpose of it. No good was realized, no life, including his own, was helped, and no real contribution was made to his environment or age. The removal of this huge stone did not send life-giving waters into a desert place, nor did it dam up some flooding disaster. This task did not dry any tears or raise any buildings for shelter or shade. It was hard work, but it as worthless. It was a painful struggle that did not reap any personal, social, civic, or vocational profit. It was an unending pointless project. It did not raise the quality of life, but it did waste a lot of time and energy. Efforts to get even steal and contaminate good quality time.

Sisyphus was not only struggling at a meaningless task, he was also struggling in hell. He didn't seem to have a choice at the point in which he was viewed. He was already in hell — doing hell's work. There was no way out! The good news for us is that we do have a way out of the hells in which we reside as a result of being treated wrongly. The best advice is not to let someone send you to hell either *here* in time or *there* in eternity. The second-best advice is to get out if you are there while you can. Resolve not to permit an ex-spouse, deceitful friend, open enemy, or jealous co-worker to become so powerful in *your* life that *you* let them lock you behind the door that keeps you struggling at a pointless task that will not make your life better.

There Is Always Too Much Left to Act as If Everything Is Gone

One of the foulest lies that satanic depression whispers to us in moments of mistreatment is that we have nothing good left. God is too merciful to leave us with nothing. If we act as if everything is gone, we kill our gratitude. The ungrateful person is always an unhappy person. The notion of a grateful person is embodied in an experience of the great theologian Matthew Henry. After having been robbed one evening, Henry went into prayer for four things: that he had never before been robbed; that he was not killed; that the thief did not take much; and that he was the one robbed and not the robber himself.

There is always something left! There is an old Hebrew legend that tells the story of a man who rode a mule. He carried with him a rooster whose crowing kept him from oversleeping. One night he entered a village. He wanted to spend the night, but the people were cruel to him and refused to let him stay in their village. He found a cave close to the village and prepared for a night's rest. A strong wind blew out his lamp so he could not read his Bible. He went into a deep sleep, and while he slept a lion ate his mule, and a wolf killed his rooster.

The next morning he arose with a faint heart but walked to the village where he had been rejected in order to purchase a meal. He found no one alive. During the night in which he slept so soundly, a band of thieves had massacred all the people and stolen their goods. As the man beheld the unhappy and tragic picture, a revelation was given and he said, "Now I understand my troubles. If the people had received me, I would have joined them in death. If my rooster and my mule had not been killed, their noise and the light from my lamp would have revealed my hiding place. God has been good to me."

There is always something left! A minister was called to serve a very poor congregation. The people were so poor, they could not afford an offering tray. The minister, at the time of the offering, passed his hat. The hat went through the congregation and returned empty! The minister, after looking at the empty hat, bowed his head and said, "Lord, I thank you I got my hat back. Amen!"

In the Greek language, there are two word which, translated into English, mean "to test." The word *dokimazo* means to test in order to approve or sanction a person or thing. The other word is *peirazo*, which means to test intentionally with the purpose of discovering weakness in a person or thing. *Peirazo* often means to test with the hope that the one put to the test will fail the test. In the Bible, *dokimazo* is generally used of God, but never of Satan. Satan never puts you to a test in order to approve you. He tests you with the hope that you will break down and fail. God tries you in order to approve you and eventually Psalm 81:16 says God will give his own "honey out of the rock." A rock is hard, but honey is sweet. Sweetness can come out of some of your hardest experiences. The sweet fellowship of the Holy Spirit is often unknown until we are placed in situations that force us to seek Him with our whole heart.

Past Favors

Yesterday's mercies were also given to us to encourage us in present and future setbacks. Gratitude flows from a memory that does not make light of the gifts that have already been. You must never permit the cruelty or indifference of people to shake loose your memories of past mercies. God is still saying what He said and doing what He did. What some see as a matter of course, wise people see as a matter of God.

The apostle Paul was a man who was often found in many trying situations. There were times when he was found without his cloak, without his books, without his friends, without his freedom. But he was never found without gratitude. The past mercies of salvation, justification, sanctification, and edification were blessings he never let slip from his memory. He had been bought, and he never forgot it. The memory of past favors cushioned his every blow and tilted the scale of every experience on the plus side.

A member of my beloved parish, Dr. Joe A. Lee, who now serves as the president of Tougaloo College in Mississippi, shared this magnificent piece of literature with me sometime ago.

A Living Faith

I've dreamed many dreams that never came true.
I've seen them vanish at dawn,
But I've realized enough of my dreams, thank God,
To make me want to dream on.

I've prayed many prayers when no answer came.
Though I waited patiently and long.
But answers have come to enough of my prayers,
To make me keep trusting on.

I've sown many seeds that fell by the way,
For the birds to feed upon.
But I've held enough golden sheaves in my hand,
To keep me sowing on.

I've drained the cup of disappointment and pain,
And gone many days without song.
But I've sipped enough nectar from the roses of life,
To make me want to live on.
I haven't accomplished every goal in life,
  as the years have come and gone.
But I've experienced enough success in my work,
To make me want to work on.

— Author Unknown

The past favors are given to keep you moving on, and if you move on, past favors are duplicated, enlarged, and sent from above as present and future gifts. No one can take from you the happiness that you already have, but you can give it up by acting as if it never happened. You can't live in the past, but you can let the good from the past undergird you as you face new trials.

"On Hold" Is Not "All Is Lost"

A lost job, a broken relationship, an undeserved demotion, as well as a host of other unforeseen and often unanticipated setbacks — have a way of making us feel that all is lost. Suspended goals distort our perspective on the future. Seeing our dreams put on hold can be difficult but not disastrous. Knowing where we want to go and being unable to get there is unsettling beyond words. *What if* and *if only* are impossible to understand unless you realize that "holding patterns" are a part of life as we live it.

When pilots reach the airport of their destination, sometimes the runway is not clear for landing. The plane might be on schedule. The pilot might have shouldered his responsibility in an admirable manner. But no matter how well the pilot has flown or how intensely the passengers want to hit the ground, if it is not safe to land, the plane is sent into a holding pattern.

In the Bible the patriarch, Joseph, was destined for greatness. He was seventeen when he had his first dream, but he was thirty before he became a ruler in Egypt. It took thirteen years for this bright, moral, and maligned "son of destiny" to realize his dreams. Joseph needed the time. He made some mistakes as a dreamer that he could not afford to make as a ruler. Joseph was anxious to tell his dreams as a dreamer, and it created problems in his own home. If he had talked about his plans as ruler as freely as he had spoken about his dreams, the security of a nation might have been jeopardized.

The pit into which Joseph was cruelly cast, the prison in which he was wrongfully placed, the envy of jealous brothers, the revenge of an unwanted woman, and the forgetfulness of an indebted butler all combined to prepare him for a royal position. Each stop along the way did something for him that made him fit for a role that might have proven too big for him prior to those events.

During many of those periods when our lives appear to be on hold, we are also being measured and fitted for greater roles. Events that add and subtract have a way of multiplying our positives and purifying our motives. They heal quick tempers, and they replace "short fuses" with a more tolerant approach to living which, of course, means a more productive lifestyle.

Mustard Seeds Can Produce Great Branches

In the New Testament, birds made their nests in trees — not in bushes. Jesus taught his disciples that the mustard seed, under the right conditions, could grow large enough to have branches in which birds would make their nests. The masses could believe that a cedar or mighty oak could house a bird's nest, but the mustard seed historically had only produced mustard bushes. The truth that our Lord wants us to grasp is that God is not limited by history. What has never been can become ordinary. The promise that transforms mustard bushes into something much greater is the same promise that God spoke in the Old Testament when he said, "I will do a new thing" (Isa. 43:19). There are times when we are required to wait patiently in order to free us from traditional and historical thinking.

The Gift of Discernment

If anyone knew about, it was the prophet Zechariah. For sixteen long years, the headstone of the temple of God lay in the ruins. When the people of God returned from seventy years of captivity in Babylon, they set out to rebuild the city of Jerusalem and its ruined temple. At the outset, they were undergirded by great expectations. They were sure that under the guidance of the Almighty, their city and their temple would soon be restored. But in this life, events often do not work out according to our schedules. Zechariah was given the gift of four prophetic visions.

A. He saw by night a man riding upon a red horse. The man stood among the myrtle trees and behind him there were red horses, speckled with white. A voice spoke saying, "We have walked to and fro through the earth, and, behold, all the earth sitteth still and is at rest" (Zech. 1:11). This vision reveals the angels of God patroling the universe. Even when life is hard and seems to be out of control, God is still in charge. You might be surprised by what has happened, but God is not! Be patient and He will prove it. Like Sarah in her old age, God will make you laugh at both your impatience and your unbelief.

B. He saw four horns and four carpenters. In the Bible a horn is always a symbol of power. The prophet saw four hostile powers. The four hostile powers worked against the people of God. They scattered them. They enslaved them. They persecuted them. But the four horns could never destroy them because there were also four carpenters in the vision. Carpenters fix things! Carpenters build things! Carpenters mend broken windows and repair leaking roofs! For every horn, there was a carpenter. For every problem, there is a divine solution. When people work against you, they also work within the limits of the divine. No matter how much your enemy does to you, he is never permitted to do more than God allows. The God who made you knows your limit. No person can destroy what God makes, and no people can defeat those that God keeps. The enemy might be strong, but God is stronger. Broken vessels can be repaired and nothing is so bad that God cannot overcome it. When you cannot — God can! There are divine carpenters ready to overcome the work of hostile powers.

The person with this gift of discernment never gives up because he knows too many reasons to keep going. Regardless of perilous threats from hostile powers the last work is always with the God who loves you more than you love yourself. God's love for you is so personal and so great that if this planet housed only you, you would be enough for Him to re-execute the holy plan of redemption.

C. He saw a man with a measuring line in his hand. The man measured the whole city of Jerusalem. This meant that the people had no further need of walls of stone. The Everlasting and Almighty God would be their wall of protection. God said, "I will be unto her a wall of fire round about and will be the glory in the midst of her" (Zech. 2:5). What God allows as trials will eventually help us. He is our protection. He directs the starry host. The winds and waves obey His will. God is a wall of fire and a light of glory. People will do cruel things to their neighbors. God protected me for my present role by permitting me to learn those lessons at an earlier date. We made vulnerable in one place in order to become invincible in another.

D. He saw two olive trees and a candlestick made of pure gold. There were seven lamps and seven pipes that fed the seven lamps. Just as the light burned from the chandelier the purposes of God continue. Delays and obstacles are a part of this life, but the purposes of God move on. Being put on hold is not mean being deserted. God is still on the throne! Jesus is still the Light of the World. It is therefore, "not by might, nor by power, but by my Spirit, saith the Lord" (Zech. 4:6).

- THREE -

NOT LUCK, BUT PROVIDENCE

In spite of what people do to us, those who seek to live victoriously must be able to speak and understand the language of God. There is, then, no such thing as luck — neither good nor bad. There are good experiences, but they do not come about as a result of good luck. There are painful, heart-breaking encounters, but they do not reach us as a result of bad luck. To soar regardless of what people do to us, we must delete the word *luck* from our vocabulary because it is not a word that is in the vocabulary of God. Whatever happens, or is prevented from happening, is a result of the providence of God. The psalmist says in Psalm 75:6-7, "For promotion cometh neither from the east, nor from the west, nor from the south, but God is the judge: he putteth down one, and setteth up another." If promotion does not come from the east, west, or south, then it must surely come from the north. Proverbs 16:33 reads, "The lot is cast into the lap; but the whole disposing thereof is of the Lord."

The true meaning *providence* is reflected in two German words. They are the words *fursehung* and *vorsehung*. The word *fursehung* means "to look out for" and the word *vorsehung* means "to see before hand." Similarly, providence is God's seeing things before they happen and making them happen for us. In His providence, God looks out for His own.

Some years ago, I was working in my office at home. My daughter, Ivy, entered and said, "Daddy, you need to take a break! I am going outside, and I need you to keep an eye on me." She felt safe and secure in the thought that my eyes were on her. She played. She ran. She rode and she jumped. Every now and then, she would look at me because somehow she knew that as I looked at her, I was also looking out for her. Providence is not only God looking at us — it is God looking out for us. We are never left alone. God is never surprised by anything or anybody because He sees all things beforehand. God exercises sovereign control over the universe and that sovereign control is called providence.

A. Preventive Providence: God by His providence prevents certain acts that would otherwise be committed. In Genesis 20:6, God said to King Abimelech, "I also withheld thee from sinning against me." Genesis 31:24 reads, "And God came to Laban the Syrian in a dream by night, and said unto him, take heed that thou speak not to Jacob either good or bad." In Hosea 2:6, God spoke, "Behold I will hedge up thy way with thorns, and make a wall, that she shall not find her paths." Sometimes God blocks a road, kills our car battery, gives us a flat tire, or changes our minds, and we do not know why. This is preventive providence at work.

B. Permissive Providence: God sees all. God knows all. God can stop anything He wants to stop, and God can start anything He sees as necessary to start. God can make mules talk, trees elect a king, and animals march two-by-two into Noah's Ark. However, God, in His wisdom, permits people to do some horrible things to us. God permitted Caesar Augustus to tax the whole world and, in His wisdom, sent His Son into the world as a helpless baby. Conventional wisdom at that hour would, without debate, forecast Caesar's impact upon the future as far greater than that of a baby born in a manger. However, Caesar perished, and that helpless baby became the Savior of the world, ruling a kingdom that has no end.

God permits the unwanted in order to produce the unlikely in a future that none can see but Him. God permits us to be in order for us to be helped and become helpful in our tomorrow. We are not simply placed in the world to live comfortable lives. Rather, to live useful lives. Just as the soil has to be plowed and turned before it yields a valuable harvest, so must be the case of the human heart. Gold only loses the impurities when it is cast into the fire. God permits us to be hurt sometimes in order for us to loosen impurities from our hearts, heads, and hands in order to make us more useful. God has big plans for us! We are not in the world merely to be blessed, we are also here to become a blessing.

The most precious words that I have heard as a pastor have been "Thank you for helping me." Through my own heartaches and disappointments, God has made me more sensitive and, therefore, more useful. I understand the fullness of gripping pain that can be experienced but not explained. My pilgrimage through such experiences have only made me wiser and more useful in tapping into those emotions in others. God has permitted me to grow in ways that no human mind can comprehend as a result of events from which I would have gladly excused myself. But that excuse would have nullified my greater state of usefulness. God did me no wrong. What He permitted made me better, and what He permits in your life will work together for good.

Occupying a position might give a person privileges and powers, but real authority comes from within, and it impacts people in life-transforming ways. Herod had a position as a king. He tried to destroy Jesus at His birth because Jesus had the authority of a king. Herod failed. What God permits will eventually clothe us with authority if we are patient. The unwanted and unpleasant will work out for our good and His glory. Otherwise, God would not have permitted it in the first place.

C. Directive Providence: Where God does not rule — He overrules. God directs the evil acts of men and women to unforeseen ends. When evil is in the heart, it will come out. God will let it come out, then will order its currents in the direction of His choosing. Joseph spoke to the very brothers who sold him into slavery saying, "As for you ye thought evil against me; but God meant it unto good, to bring to pass, as it is this day, to save much people alive" (Gen. 50:20). The trip to Egypt meant one thing to Joseph's brothers, but another to God. Joseph's humiliation transformed into exaltation. God directs the currents. He over-rules evil purposes even when He allows the evil act. The theme of usefulness appears here "to save much people alive." Joseph was chosen to be a savior for a starving people in a time of famine. His coat of many colors and his residence in his father's tent had no place in his future. God directed the currents that carried him to a seat that saved a nation.

D. Determinative Providence: God determines the boundaries reached by evil. God measures the effects, and calculates the extent to which the act can go. Job 38:11 says, "Hitherto, shalt thou some, but no further: and here shall thy proud waves be stayed?" God was answering a suffering man with a question that has no human answer. The question of where we were at the time the Almighty drew the boundaries of the waters upon the shores, only summons each of us to say with Job, "Therefore have I uttered that I understood not" (Job 42:3). God draws a line that no enemy can cross. Even when we are tempted the apostle Paul tells us, "God will not suffer you to be tempted above that ye are able; but will with the temptation also make the way of escape that ye may be able to endure it" (1 Cor. 10:13). God might not stop an enemy from sabotaging your plans, but God determines how far the sabotage can go. Whatever is taken is only taken in order to make room for something better. The Matterhorn is a mountain located on the Italian-Swiss border. The mountain, is 14,692 feet high. It was in this high place, where no human life had residence, that a few mountain lovers took a vacation. One of the vacationers caught a tiny fly and examined it under a pock-et microscope. They discovered that this tiny fly which resembled other ordinary flies, had its legs thickly covered with small hairs to keep it warm. If the kindness of God would put hair on a fly to keep it comfortable on an icy mountain, how much more kindness will He show to those made by Him in order that they may know Him. If God was careful to put hair on the legs of a fly, He will surely be careful to determine the boundaries of the evils that hurt us.

Reached, But Not Ruled

If an evil act against you rules you, it will eventually make you into what it is or something quite similar. God permits evil against you for your future good and for His eventual glory. God determines the limits of what the act does to your external life, but you decide what it can do to you internally. If you allow the evil done to you to shape you, you will abort your heavenly intention and, in a sense, submit yourself to the wrong doer. If God permits the act to reach you, He will give you the strength to manage it.

Evil committed against you gives you a chance to demonstrate your greatness. Petty and vindictive people remove themselves out for any inclusion into the number of those that might be labeled as great in the eyes of God or man. There is nothing good in revenge.

Evil committed against you is designed in the economy of God to *serve* you and not to *rule* you. All evil, including our own meets its match in the presence of God. Your enemy wins a great victory when you stop hating hate and start loving love. Resisting evil men and base instincts takes much prayer, patience, and the power that comes from a rich faith that can stand to be tested. It is not easy, but it is possible to remain calm under fire. When we fail to subdue our anger, we risk losing some of the greatest blessings in our lives.

I am not advocating a passive "kick me" approach. This would only invite further abuse. I am saying, however, "be ye angry and sin not." We have a choice to become retaliatory or victorious. The victorious thrust is a combination of common sense and calm assurance that refuses to become a victim to be ruled by an enemy. Meekness is "strength under control." We must, especially during periods when we are hurt, work to make evil actions against us our servants rather than our rulers. People might break your heart, but they cannot destroy your future without your cooperation. Be ruled by a passion to be productive, happy, and useful. Be served by the unpleasant by permitting it to be a striking illustration of all that you choose not to be. Ignoring is most effective with those behaviors which have previously been nurtured by attention. The worst reaction you can provide for a troublemaker is to give that person the attention that has no negative consequence. If this matter can be ignored, it ought to be, and whatever it is that you ought to do, you can do. Proverbs 16:32 says, "He that is slow to anger is better than the mighty; and he that ruleth his spirit than he that taketh a city."

God Has a Hedge and an Armor for His Own

If you are a child of God, nobody can touch you without God's permission. There is a spiritual hedge of divine protection around you and yours. You are not on your own, therefore, you do not have the total responsibility of taking care of yourself. I am glad that this is the case because I have learned that I cannot take care of myself alone. As a matter of fact, I cannot even put my arms around myself, and neither can you. We can, however, maintain fellowship with the eternal One who knows the roads we travel, the turns we must take, the stops we must make, and even the detours. God knows both our permanent address and our temporary locations, and He has determined to protect us in mysterious ways. The power of this truth is dramatized in the Old Testament story of Job.

The Book of Job teaches us some important lessons about how events in heaven affect situations here on earth. It is hard to grasp, but Satan has access to heaven and earth. Many of us like to think that Satan is living in hell most of the time, and that he skips out, does his thing, and has to return. This is not what the Bible teaches. Satan is a rebellious angel with limitations placed on him only by God. Job 1:6 says, "Now there was a day when the sons of God came to present themselves before the Lord, and Satan came also among them." Satan had stalked Job. He slandered both God and Job. Satan accused Job of having a commercial faith. He was saying that Job only served God because of the blessings he had received and that Job was willing to sell out his praises to the highest bidder. The charge against God was even more serious. He was saying that God is not worthy to be worshiped because of *who* He *is* and that God was being worshiped simply because of what He *does.*

Satan hated the fellowship that Job enjoyed with God. He had watched it and resented it. He wanted to sever it, but he could not touch Job. God had put something around Job, around his house, around his children, around his livestock in the fields, and around his investments at the markets. Satan could not touch him, and he cannot touch you as long as that something, that power, that hedge surrounds you. People may want to do you wrong. They might look for a chance, wait for an opportunity, create a crisis, but none can touch you without God's permission! The hedge is up! You cannot buy it. You cannot earn it. The hedge is a gift from a loving Father to His children simply because it is a father's nature to protect. No person is truly protected who is not protected by God. Satan is not intimidated by our security alarm systems. He is not fearful of our police departments. He is not fearful of our police departments. He is not limited by our fences. He is not excluded by our politics or finances, and no human weapon, no earth-born army, no laser technology, no thrust from the hands of flesh and blood trouble him. He is the devil. The word devil comes from the Greek words *Dia-Ballo* which means "to throw across." The devil is a spirit. He can climb over any of our fences. He can crash our markets. He can sabotage our computers. He can taint our medication. He is a devil. He is always throwing something across our paths. He can break down *our* barriers but he cannot touch us behind God's hedge.

In His wisdom, God gave Satan the shears. He permitted him to cut down the hedge, but He never permitted Satan to take away Job's armor. When the hedge is taken away the armor of God will hold up. No matter how strongly you feel that you have been deserted, you have not. The hedge may seem cut for a while but the armor will hold. The night might seem long, but "joy cometh in the morning." If God sends the storm, He will guide the ship. The "passage may not be smooth" but "the landing will be safe" because the armor of God will hold up. First Corinthians 10:13 says, "There hath no temptation taken you but such as is common to man: but God is faithful, who will not suffer you to be tempted above that ye are able; but will with the temptation also make a way to escape, that ye may be able to bear it." God knows just how much we can bear. He draws the limits. Satan might swing the hammer, but God determines the impact.

Job lost health, wealth, and family but the Bible says in Job 42:12 "So the LORD blessed the latter end of Job more than his beginning." He lost five hundred donkeys — he ended up with a thousand. He lost five hundred oxen — he ended up with a thousand. He lost three thousand camels — he ended up with six thousand. He lost seven thousand sheep — he ended up with fourteen thousand. He buried ten children — he was given ten more and ended up with twenty children. Ten children were in God's house and ten were in his house. God doubled everything that he had. While we do not see the present benefits of God's testing, the outcome is always greater than we can imagine.

- FOUR -

TREASURES OUT OF DARKNESS

There is no person and no circumstance that is beyond the influence of God. If you can grasp this truth, you will be saved from worrying yourself. Someone once said, "Worry is like rocking in a rocking chair — it will give you something to do, but it will not get you anywhere." In the previous chapter we have refuted the theory of blind fate and luck. During a troubling period in his life, David spoke in Psalm 31:15 saying, "My times are in thy hand: deliver me from the hand of mine enemies, and from them that persecute me." If our times are in the hands of God, then our days and our darkest nights reside there as well. We are never beyond the care of our Maker, and our difficult periods are scripted into a divinely written play that can have nothing less than a glorious ending. But prior to destination there are uncounted treasures that are mounted against a seemingly starless night.

God Has a Better Plan

God is a God of planning. There are times when something as annoying and unspiritual as a broken leg serves as a gateway to an unmeasured blessing. Bernard Gilpin was accused of heresy during the Middle Ages. He was called to appear in London, England, from his home in Scotland. His trial was set before Bishop Bonner. Being a spiritual man with deep biblical roots, he had a favorite saying which was, "All things are for the best." He was brave and unashamed of his beliefs. He was willing to speak for himself in spite of consequences. He feared God and in fearing God, he lost the fear of everything and everyone else. When he received the summons, he set out on his journey. On the journey to London, he broke his leg. A guard who had no appreciation for his faith jested and asked, "Now that you are laid up do you still think that all things are for the best?" He replied in the affirmative. He did not know how right he was. He was laid up and therefore was unable to travel for a while. While he rested his broken leg, things were happening. The queen who hated him, died. The bishop who planned to destroy him was replaced. Instead of going to London to be burned at the stake, he went there to receive a great honor and experience a victory that was won for him while he was enduring the misery of a broken leg. The broken leg only restricted him during the time God's plan intended. We might make some good plans, but God always hands out a better plan.

Disappointment is a down-to-earth experience that greets each of us. What we do with the disappointment is what separates us. Sometimes our goals are vetoed by the wisdom and love of the Eternal. No purpose is explained; no reason will be given; no revelation will surface; and stress will enfeeble us, unless we confront that disappointment with the right ideas about God. God is too good to leave us alone. He is too merciful to throw us out. He has a plan. Some of it will be revealed, and all of it will be executed for our good. God supports us by His grace, and He tries us according to His wisdom in order to mature, enrich, and empower us for greater purposes. Our plans might be good, but God's plan is always better. We are not simply God's allies; we are also His agents through which he shines a bright light in the darkest.

When people seek to hurt you, they are often dropping ingredients into a recipe that will spell success according to God's plan. The formula for that success escalates from myriad human efforts. "He who hates me teaches me caution and he who is indifferent to me teaches me self-reliance." The person who hates you intends to do many things except teach you a skill that will bless your days and brighten your hours. The person who is indifferent to you certainly does not project a goal to teach you ways to become self-reliant.

Trust is a powerful weapon when it is rightly focused. When it is unwisely placed, it locks you out of the race. Trust and belief have similarities, but are different. One can believe in God and one can trust in God. When you believe in someone you might risk a little but not a lot. You would not give your car keys to people you believe in as readily as you would to people you trust. The same principle applies to God. You can believe in God, but belief alone will not give you the same power that comes as a result of trusting God. We learn to trust as a result of getting to know the person who solicits our trust. It comes as a result of finding the object worthy of our trust. Our trust in God's plan being superior to ours depends upon our reaction to the plan itself.

You Can Catwalk God's Plan

A catwalk is a narrow pathway. Our response to God's greatness can be a narrow response. God desires fullness for us. I recall hearing a story about a man who lived in New York City. He spent his entire adult life in an area that included the shop where he worked, the market where he shopped, and a few blocks from the apartment that he rented. This man never saw a Broadway play. He never attended a professional sporting event. He never graced the hall of any of the city's museums, nor did he jog through any of the attractive parks. He lived in New York, but he catwalked his experience.

God had a great plan that included a taste of the world for the apostle Peter. However, Peter was hemmed in by history. God moved in the heart of a Roman centurion by the name of Cornelius. Cornelius was a devout man. He was kind, spiritual, and open-hearted, but he was without a full revelation of God's plan of salvation. God gave him a vision that included Peter, but Peter almost missed his chance to expand his ministry. Peter was a prisoner of history rather than an instrument of redemption. He was catwalking the plan until he went "upon the housetop to pray." Acts 10:10-20 relates the vision that unshackled him.

> *And he became very hungry, and would have eaten: but while they made ready, he fell into a trance, and saw heaven opened, and a certain vessel descending unto him, as it had been a great sheet knit at the four corners, and let down to the earth: wherein were all manner of four footed beasts of the earth, and wild beasts, and creeping things, and fouls of the air. And there came a voice to him, rise, Peter; kill, and eat. But Peter said, not so, Lord; for I have never eaten anything that is common or unclean. And the voice spake unto him again the second time, what God hath cleansed, that call not thou common. This was done thrice: and the vessel was received up again into heaven. Now while Peter doubted in himself what this vision which he had seen should mean, behold, the men which were sent from Cornelius had made inquiry for Simon's gate, and called, and asked whether Sinon, which was surnamed peter, were lodged there. While peter thought on the vision, the spirit said unto him, behold, three men seek thee. Arise therefore, and get thee down, and go with them, doubting nothing; for I have sent them.*

Peter was not at his permanent residence. He was just stopping by Simon's house. God always knows where we are. He knows where we are emotionally, mentally, spiritually, and physically, even when our condition is only temporary. We are all going somewhere with God. We can go walking like Enoch, who walked with God, or we can go kicking, screaming, and crying. Regardless of posture, we are going to be set in motion. God is not limited by history. He does not need our delineation of our history. When He reveals the plan, we must be open and respond accordingly. Catwalking only postpones our blessings.

You Can Cooperate With God's Plan

There is a beautiful painting by an artist by the name of Diego Rivera. the painting is called *The Flower Vender*. In the painting, an elderly peasant is seen leaving home for the market. He is on his knees and leaning forward. His wife is seen assisting him. She is placing a large basket packed with beautiful flowers on his back. The picture of cooperation is driven home forcefully. These two elderly people working together get the job done. God loves us enough to give us a choice. We can cooperate with his designs and get the job done, or we can resist at the risk our own peril and ultimate discomfort.

Cooperating with God's plan is not just "going along for the ride." Lot was the nephew of Abraham who left Ur of Chaldees looking for the city of God. Lot was just looking. And when you are just looking, you fall for those outer appearances that look good.

Sometimes the wrongs committed against you will force you into a closer walk with God. There are some wounds that cut so deeply only God can heal them, and as He heals you, He also matures you. As God matures you, He frees you for a committed relationship. Walking by faith is a deliberate act. In days of yore, the story goes that dishonest farmers who were prone to make a quick dollar would stuff a squirming cat into a sack. They would tie the top of the sack securely, then they would offer the bag up to an unsuspecting shopper as a plump, young pig. If the customer became suspicious enough to open the sack and check out the merchandise, he was said to "let the cat out of the bag." If, on the other hand, he was trusting, he was said to "buy a pig in a poke." Faith in God is not a call to gullibility.

Long before the first farmer dropped the first squirming cat into a bag, a young man by the name of Jacob bought his own pig in a poke. Jacob was clever. He had business acumen. God had chosen Jacob for great things, but Jacob decided not to wait on God. He took matters into his own hands and made an irrevocable mess. He ended up living with the consequences of scheming behavior. He went to what he thought was the right wedding, but he married the wrong bride. God could have let "the cat out of the bag," but when we leave God out of our plans, we are left, at least for a while, to make it on our own. Jacob was born in a religious setting. He had even had a religious experience at a place called Bethel. It is possible to be religious but not spiritual. Going along for the ride can get us to the right place without getting us right for the place.

You Can Activate God's Plan

Sometimes God wants to do something in us, through us, and even for us, but we are not ready. It took forty years for God's people to reach a land that they could have occupied in forty days.

Recently, I held an intense but very productive counseling session with an attractive young woman who had been jilted by someone with whom she had been in love for a long time. At one point in our session, she asked, through tear-stained eyes, "How long will it take me to get over this?" My response initially shocked her when I said, "As long as you want it to take." It is not God's will that we waste one hour. God's design makes no plan for our self-imposed isolation. We are never chosen to hurt for the sake of hurting. Our hurts are designed to be our helps. However, it is up to us to determine how long it will take before the transformation occurs.

God has a purpose for every drop of water. It never rains too much according to the master plan. No baby is really born before time and no person lives too long. Between the wood of the cradle and the marble of the grave, we can speed up recovery or we can lengthen our sorrow. There is a clear illustration of this truth listed in Exodus 8:6-10.

> *And Aaron stretched out his hand over the waters of Egypt; and the frogs came up, and covered the land of Egypt. And the magicians did so with their enchantments, and brought up frogs upon the land of Egypt. Then Pharaoh called for*

Moses and Aaron, and said, entreat the Lord, that he may take away the frogs from me, and from my people; and I will let the people go, that they may do sacrifice unto the Lord. And Moses said unto Pharaoh, glory over me: when shall I entreat for thee, and for thy servants, and for thy people, to destroy the frogs from thee and thy houses, that they may remain in the river only? And he said tomorrow. And he said, be it according to thy word: that thou mayest know that there is none like unto the Lord over God.

It has always appeared strange to me that Pharaoh postponed the departure of the frogs. When the question was asked by Moses as to when should he approach God for relief, Pharaoh said tomorrow. Why he did not request immediate relief is a puzzle to me. Why did he not simply say today or tonight? Pharaoh said, "Do it tomorrow." Moses said, "Fine, I will do it according to your timetable." Deliverance could have taken place immediately. Pharaoh lengthened his agony and the agony of his people.

God's plan is steadily progressing, and He is waiting for us to willingly move ahead with Him.

- FIVE -

DEFENDING THE WHEAT FROM THE TARES

When people wrong you, your real friends will rise to your comfort. It will become self-evident who does not love you. This is good. You need to know the difference. This does not mean that you have to do anything or say anything. You just need to know who you can trust and who you had better not trust. There are some people that must be categorized with the counterfeit not because of their intentions but because of their weaknesses. The story of the three ministers on a weekend camping trip is my focus here in a humorous, yet truthful manner. The three ministers were isolated from the pressures of deadlines, debates, congregations, and other church responsibilities. As they shared their hopes, they decided to share their weaknesses. The first to share his vulnerability revealed a weakness for alcohol. The second confessor admitted to being a kleptomaniac. The third minister sat back absorbing it all like a sponge, and when the others required his confession, he replied, "I am a gossiper and I must confess, I cannot wait to get back to town." Self-disclosure is a must for some relationships, but it is a disaster for some interactions. There are some that you cannot trust. Blessed is the experience or person that teaches you the difference.

In Matthew 13:24-30, our Lord converted a parable into an allegory for the purpose of interpretation.

Another parable put he forth unto them, saying, the kingdom of heaven is likened unto a man which sowed good seed in his field: but while men slept, his enemy came and sowed tares among the wheat, and went his way. But when the blade was sprung up, and brought forth fruit, then appeared the tares also. So the servants of the householder came and said unto him, sir, didst not thou sow good seed in thy field? From whence then hath it tares? He said unto them, an enemy hath done this. The servants said unto him, wilt thou then that we go and gather them up? But he said, nay; lest while ye gather up the tares, ye root up also the wheat with them. Let both grow together until the harvest and in the time of harvest I will say to the reapers, gather ye together first the tares, and bind them in bundles to burn them: but gather the wheat into my barn."

The good seed refers here to the godly. The tares refer to those that look godly but are not. The tares were counterfeit wheat. The man in the parable represents the person who is trying to live a Christian life. He represents that person who really wants to be a good, decent, hardworking contributor. This type of person should have prospered without having to confront certain unsettling realities, but this just did not happen. He went to sleep after a hard day's labor, and while he slept, an enemy went to work. The enemy's work was deliberate. It was quick, and it was quiet. As a matter of fact, the ruinous work was done so cleverly that nobody suspected it until months later. By this time the root system between the darnel (tares) and wheat were intertwined. You couldn't pull up the bad without ripping up the good and destroying the change for a good harvest crop.

While our Lord said, "Don't try to separate." He never said, "Don't learn the difference." In our families, on our jobs, in our churches, among our many relationships, there are often more tares than wheat. It is not your task to separate, but it is in your best interest to discern the difference and be wise enough to avoid self-disclosure to those unworthy of your trust.

Be Alert

Martin Luther, categorized by history with the stamp of greatness, spoke an insightful parable on the subject of remaining alert. In his parable Luther pictured a council convened in hell. Satan presided and demons competed for a prize for the best infernal service performed by a devil. According to Luther, one contestant said, "I saw a caravan of weary travelers crossing a heated desert. I called on the Sirocco with its hot and foul breath. I whirled the sandy masses and blotted out the heavens. I buried their bones in a sandy grave." Satan replied, "Well done, but a greater work can be done."

Another competitor spoke up. He said, "I watched a gallant life-laden vessel skimming the surface of a glassy sea. I hissed from a distance for a roaring tempest. I piled a mountain of foaming surge on the deck. the ship went down with a sullen plunge and now the deep waters have claimed a whole ship load." Satan bowed in approval saying, "Well done, but still a greater work could have been done."

Finally, that last demon appeared. He raised his voice with a chuckle of conscious triumph and said, "I went to church. I saw a congregation blessed by God engaged in a revival. Souls were being won to Christ. the choirs were singing with power. The preacher was preaching with unction. The breath of the Lord blew. The congregation praised the Lord as a mighty host, but I went to work. I substituted material good for spiritual fervor. I put money in the treasury. I sent my crowd and filled the pews to standing room only. I gave the preacher popularity. I gave the congregation success and now the minister and the members have all gone to sleep." Satan stood up and said, "The prize is thine for this is the greatest work!" A sleeping church takes nothing and makes nothing. The work of God has to be done by active hands and busy feet.

We must be able to recognize the effects of evil around us, but we cannot retaliate with hatred, against those who intend to harm us. You must not hate them for hate is a poison, and poison kills. Alex Haley, the author of *Roots*, once said, "Hate at its best will distance you; at its worst, it will destroy you; but it will always immobilize you." You must never allow yourself to be enslaved by hate, yet you must be, in the language of our Lord, "wise as a serpent." I am amazed at the fact that snakes live, slither, and operate for most of their lives in the dust, yet I have never seen a dirty snake. Somehow the serpent who lives in the dust finds a way to repel the dirt. You can remain free evil influences even as you deal with evil doers, but you must develop and maintain a formula that keeps your heart dirt-free. The psalmist teaches us that, "If I regard iniquity in my heart thou [God] will not hear my prayer" (Psalm 66:18).

Be Attentive

Don't just *look* at what happens to you, *study* it as well. Nothing takes the place of serious study. Mental concentration is a necessity if you are going to distinguish the difference between the real and the counterfeit people who affect your life. Just as a rattle snake rattles prior to striking, there are often many warning signals that come from counterfeit people. Do not overreact to the noise of the rattler, but do not ignore it, either. Listen, study, and try to be certain that what you hear or see is truly a signal. If you are able to define the source of danger without the source knowing what you know, you are ahead of the game.

In the sixteenth chapter of the book of Judges, Samson clearly had the upper hand on Delilah, but he made the mistake of not using the knowledge he had gained. He tested Delilah with the wrong information and she failed both tests. If a person can harm you with the wrong information, How much more can they with that which is accurate. Instead of becoming a wise student, Samson became a sad victim. He did not study. He saw what happened as he explained that his strength could be overcome "with seven green withes that were never dried" and being bound with "new ropes that were never occupied." At each revelation Delilah acted. The King James Version of the Bible tells us that "she bound him." He knew what hap happened. He felt it. He experienced it, but he failed to study it.

Being tied up by the person with whom he shared his secret should have sent Samson's guard up. But he did not think. He did not attend, and he did not interpret. The real people in your life seek to make you strong. The people who love you do not find enjoyment in seeing you weak. The dialogue between Samson and Delilah was one about strength and weakness. You must be careful in expounding any source of your strength that can be managed or manipulated by flesh and blood. Strength over-extended can become weakness. Samson lost his ability to attend to the events that he was experiencing. He revealed the true symbol of his strength, and Delilah used it against him.

The real comrade seeks your good by working to make themselves channels through which your strength is maximized. Job 4:3-4 states, "Behold, thou hast instructed many, thou hast strengthened the weak hands. Thy words have upholden him that was falling, and thou hast strengthened the feeble knees."

True friends seek to keep you on your feet. They see nothing good in tying you up in order to measure your weakness. They share their struggles with you in order to make you strong, rather than marketing their strengths to cancel your hope. This is dramatically illustrated in the work of Langston Hughes as he records advice from "Mother to Son" about surviving the struggles of life.

The people who are encouraging you in mediocrity and complacency are counterfeit people who are comparing themselves and competing with your achievements. They do not want to do better; they just want you to stop moving ahead of where they see themselves. "Wisdom is not in words but in meanings within the words" (Kahil Gilbran), of those who surround and confront you.

The counterfeit people in your life will be envious even of your least achievements. Envious people who are close to you ought to be recognized as soon as possible and confided in with caution. There is a Hebrew legend that depicts the insanity of envy. According to the legend, two Hebrew merchants were located across the street from one another. No matter how well business was for each man, the other was miserable if his competitor surpassed him. They engaged in price wars to the point that each would lost profits on items that both sold, simply for the sake of pulling customers away from the other.

God grew weary of their pettiness and sent an angel with an offer which should have ended the rivalry. The offer was made to the merchant who was most vocal. He was given the option of asking for anything, and it would be granted. However, no matter how much he received his rival would receive double. If he receive on hundred pearls; his rival would receive two hundred pearls. The man thought for a while and a smile came upon his face. The angel prepared himself to bless the man when he said, "I know exactly what I want. make me blind in one eye."

Because of envy, he chose a curse and threw away a fortune. Be attentive as you deal wisely with the envious people in your life. It has been said, "If you are beautiful at age sixteen, it is a gift of God, but if you are not beautiful at age sixty, it's your own fault." Be attentive, grow, and glow in spite of, and at times even because of, the unkindness of others.

– Six –

VENGEANCE BELONGS TO GOD

It has been said that "God might not pay off every week, but he does pay off." I was especially moved with a story that I heard a few years ago about a farmer who did not believe in God. I have long felt that farmers should be believers simply because they have to depend on God in a unique way that affects their occupation. They plant, but God alone manages the germination process. God sends the right amount of rain knowing that too much is as disastrous as too little.

According to a story, there was one farmer who did not credit God with having dispensed any favors. He worked his crops on Sunday and told his fellow neighbors that his harvest would be as bountiful or more so than theirs. At harvest time, he displayed an excellent crop. He boasted and asked his God-fearing neighbor for a response. The godly neighbor replied, "The only thing I can say is that God doesn't settle all of his accounts in October." He was right! God has both a plan to settle matters with perfect equity, with perfect justice, and with perfect timing.

When God Writes the Script, the Ending
Is Sometimes Surprising

The apostle Paul wrote in Romans 12:19, "Dearly beloved, avenge not yourselves, but rather give place unto wrath: for it is written, Vengeance is mine; I will repay, saith the Lord." If you are always defending yourself, the Lord is never given a chance to defend you. If you are busy taking vengeance, then you are trying to use God's authority and compromising God's chance to vindicate you. You will, by taking vengeance, create a condition that will add to your sorrow. There is a magnificent story by Geoffrey Farnol, which dramatizes this truth. In this story Martin Conisby was an heir to a great estate. he was also a victim of a nasty feud, which had dragged on for hundreds of years, between his family and their neighbors whose name was Brandon.

Richard Brandon killed Martin's father and arranged for Martin to be sold as a slave on a Spanish vessel. As Martin suffered in his role as a slave, confined to rowing the massive vessel, he often prayed, "O God of justice, for the agony I needs must now endure, for the bloody stripes and bitter anguish give me vengeance, O, God, on mine enemy." We need to be careful and selective in our praying. Some of the things we request may well be the least of things that will fit well into our future. Martin eventually escaped his enslavement and set out to get his revenge on his hated enemy.

The story weaves its way into a dungeon during the time of the Spanish Inquisition. To get revenge Martin Conisby has himself arrested by officers of the inquisition because he hears that his enemy Richard Brandon is imprisoned in the dungeons. He goes to the dungeon with the hope that he can be placed in the same cell with his enemy. He found his enemy, in the dirt and darkness of a foul dungeon. But what he found was not what he expected. Sir Richard was an old, beaten, withered, and broken creature. His body had "many grievous scars of wounds, old and new, the marks of hot and searing iron, of biting steel and cruel lash, and in joints swollen and inflamed, he read the oft-repeated torture of the rack."

Martin had come looking for a strong man upon whom he could wreak his hate and satisfy his thirst for retribution. He found someone different. Sir Richard had been broken in body but ennobled by his pain. The two men who had been bitter enemies became more than friends. Sir Richard found a son, and Martin found a man whom he loved as a father. They escaped together and fled across the wild wastes of Darien. Sir Richard died on their journey to the sea, and Martin wept for a man he both loved and honored. Vengeance is best handled by God. God sees what we cannot see, and He avenges wrong with a wisdom that is as high above us as "the heavens are above the earth."

When God Writes the Script, the Ending Is Always Just

Many years ago in Talladega, Alabama, I am told that a great tragedy took place, which wreaks of both human misunderstanding and human injustice. A small girl was playing in a yard. She was attacked by wasps. The child wept, screamed, and ran, only to make matters worse. A man happened by and took notice of the incident. He caught the child, rolled her in the grass to free her from the wasps that had gotten in her clothing. As the man worked frantically to save the child, the child's father emerged from the house. He heard the child crying. He saw the man bending over the child. The father misread what was happening, went back into the house, returned with a gun, and killed a man who was trying to save his daughter. I relate this story to remind you that sometimes you cannot trust what you think you see. We are finite. God is infinite. While we cannot always trust ourselves, we can always trust God to do what is just in the end because He says, "I will repay."

There is a difference between human weakness and human wickedness. The difference is always found in the heart. "The heart of the problem is the problem of the heart." We cannot speak with authority on the issues of the heart and the judgments that are warranted. But God offers the first word and demands the last word. He is eternal and He is always just. Evil will not stand. Evil doers will not stand. Evil can never have ultimate victory over good. What God writes will stand forever.

The Handwriting of the Eternal Is Always Just at the End

A. Adoni-Bezek (Judges 1:4-7): This man was a Canaanite king who turned his palace into an insane asylum. He mutilated seventy kings. He cut off their thumbs and their big toes. Without thumbs, their hands became claws, and without big toes, it was difficult for them to maintain their balance. They were rationed food and herded into the palace dining area where the food was thrown under the table. They had to eat from the floor.

God's Vengeance: Adoni-Bezek was defeated by the tribe of Judah. He ran but was captured. They cut off his thumbs and big toes. His conscience rebuked him. He said, "Threescore and ten kings, having their thumbs and their great toes cut off, gathered their meat under my table: as I have done, so God hath requited me. And they brought him to Jerusalem, and there he died."

B. The Brothers of Joseph, "The Dreamer": They hated him and their hostility escalated into violence. They threw him into a pit, stained his coat of many colors, and sold him into slavery. Sometimes people (even family members) will resent you for gifts that you have no control over. Those who share a common heritage with you will sometimes resent you intensely when they feel that they cannot share a common destiny with you. God gave Joseph great dreams. The very dreams that were the source of his trouble also foretold his triumph.

God's Vengeance: Somewhere I read a statement which says, "The sweetest form of revenge is becoming successful." The Bible tells about Joseph who was convicted on trumped-up charges by an envious woman. God raised him up without Joseph taking vengeance. He ascended the throne and exercised great authority. The same brothers who wronged him became helpless and arrived in his presence in a needy condition. Across the years I have seen God humble people in this manner. Sometimes the wrong-doers find themselves on a sick bed, and the only person to give them a glass of cold water is the person they mistreated at an earlier time. God seems to use this method not only to humble the wrong-doer, but also to test the person who has been wronged. It will not be unusual, when people have wronged you, to find them helpless and knocking on your door.

Joseph forgave his brothers with a Christlike compassion. You cannot nurture growth and grudges in the same heart. One will destroy the other. Spiritual growth will make you too big to wear a grudge. And if you nurture your grudge, it will shrink your soul, dim your vision, and limit your future.

C. Cain: He was the world's first murderer. He killed his brother Abel. Cain was a religious man, yet he killed his brother. Religion can be the best or the worst influence in a person's life. The wrong kind of religion can intensify cruelty. In Cain, the evil of envy appeared in all of its deadly rage. Both Cain and Abel offered sacrifices to God. Cain was rejected, not because God loved him less, but because something was wrong with his offering. It was not acceptable, and his spirit polluted it. Abel had nothing to do with it. The rejection problem was between Cain and God. Cain killed his brother and buried him only to have to face God.

God's Vengeance: Just as Cain had surveyed his altar, God had surveyed his murderous act. God replied, "The voice of thy brother's blood crieth unto me from the ground . . . a fugitive and a vagabond shalt thou be in the earth." He was lost. He was cursed. He would never be able to rest. Peace would always elude him. His life would be meaningless and spoiled. His energies would be drained and his traveling shoes would always be pointed away from God. He feared what people would do to him, yet it did not trouble him that he was enmeshed in something that pursued a fearful lifestyle.

D. David: David was not an evil man, but he did commit an evil deed against Uriah the Hittite (2 Sam. 11:18).

"Then Joab sent and told David all the things concerning the war."

1. David Wronged His Army. The Israelite nation wanted a king to lead them in battle (1 Sam. 8:20). The army was out fighting at the siege of Rabbah. King David remained at the palace. He had idle time upon the roof of his palace and saw the beautiful Bathsheba taking a bath. Had David lived up to his responsibility, he would not have been in the palace on the day in which he first lusted after Bathsheba, the wife of Uriah the Hittite.

2. David Wronged Bathsheba (2 Sam. 11:4). As king in the day in which david lived, this was no great wrong to the minds of many, yet David's conscience seemed to have pricked him. The Bible says, "David sent messengers and took her." She had no say in the matter. She was more of a victim than a partner in an age and culture that often determined the worth of a woman according to the men she had in her life.

3. David Wronged Uriah (2 Sam. 11:15). David knew which buttons to push and which strings to pull. He arranged for a frontline battle assignment. David's words were, "Set ye Uriah in the forefront of the hottest battle, and retire ye from him, that he may be smitten, and die." David's orders were not only given to assign but also to abandon.

God's Vengeance: David destroyed a family. God's grace forgave him when he repented, but God's government repaid him in kind. Frederick Douglass was speaking at an anti-slavery meeting in a hall at Salem, Ohio. He felt defeated. His voice sounded out a note of pessimism. Sojourner Truth was at the same meeting. She spoke out from the gallery, "Frederick, Frederick, is God dead?" God was not dead, and His government was not dysfunctional. David's family was riddled with tragedy. 2 Samuel 12:10 says, "Now therefore the sword shall never depart from thine house; because thou hast despised me, and hast taken the wife of Uriah the Hittite to be thy wife."

1. The Lord struck the child that Bathsheba bore. David knew that his child's sickness was a judgment from God. At the death of the child, David spoke the famous words, "I shall go to him, but he shall not return to me."

2. Amnon, the son of David, raped his sister Tamar.

3. Absalom, another son of David, avenged his sister, Tamar and killed his half-brother Amnon. It took two years before Absalom was able to carry out his plot for revenge.

4. Absalom was banished, eventually led a rebellion against david, and died as a young man on the run.

Those who harm others deserve our pity rather than our anger.

E. Haman (Esther 7:1-10): Haman was a man with a great position. He was the chief minister of King Ahasuerus of Persia when Persia was a powerful nation. Despite his position and power, Haman hated Esther's cousin Mordecai because he refused to bow before him. Haman developed a scheme to destroy Mordecai that eventually led to his own personal undoing.

As a child I often heard this statement that was meant to focus upon the value of kindness and the danger of treacherous living.

"If you dig one ditch, you'd better dig two —
The one you dig for me just might be for you."

This truth is clearly delineated in the tragic story of Haman. Haman was enraged because Mordecai refused to bow to him so he called for the extermination of Mordecai and all of his people. Haman used his powerful position to misrepresent the Jews. If you will recall, I mentioned earlier that persecutors seek to misrepresent the persecuted in order to carry out their evil doing.

There are many ways to operate in the dark, of which the clocks on the wall and the position of sun, moon, and stars have no bearing. Haman created an ominous climate for Mordecai. Haman did not know that his plan to destroy Mordecai would also destroy the queen of the kingdom, Esther.

God's Vengeance: The providence of God moved. Esther was given a more prominent place than haman. She was the queen, and she was also the cousin of Mordecai. Haman was so certain of his success that he offered to pay about twenty million dollars to cover the cost of his plan and built a seventy-five foot gallows on which to hang Mordecai. God refused to let the king sleep on the very night Haman was putting the finishing touches on his plan. The restless king sent for his book of memorable deeds. While reading the book he discovered that Mordecai had exposed a plot to take his life and had never been rewarded. While Haman was looking for a way to destroy, the king began searching for a way to reward.

Esther gave a banquet, and the king attended. She exposed the plot. Haman begged for her forgiveness. As the king returned to Queen Esther's side, Haman fell upon the couch where she was sitting. The king thought Haman was assaulting Esther and immediately sentenced him to death. Haman was hanged from his own gallows. Thus, God allowed this man to perish from the works of his own hands.

F. Jezebel and Ahab (1 Kings 21; 2 Kings 9): When you have love, you can be happy, even with a little; but if you do not have love, you cannot be happy, no matter how much you have. Ahab was a king in name only. He sold himself to a spirit of covetousness and sacrificed his future.

As I write this section, I recall the capture of a man from my community who was listed for several years on the FBI's "Most Wanted" list. The man's name is Larry Donald George. He was charged with murder, and had been a fugitive for several years. He was captured in New Castle County, Delaware, on the Christina River. It seems that this man who is charged for murder, stole and struggled against the elements for two or three years, in that area. He survived by existing in a five- to six-foot wide, twelve-foot long, dwelling, under a mound of trash. To exist in a trash pile, this man broke into homes and even carried a generator for several miles. To exist in a trash pile, this man worked, struggled, and ran. He had a television set, a VCR, clothing, a new pair of Nike shoes, food, magazines, and newspapers at the time of his arrest. Some people considered him clever, but the fact that he was living under a mound of trash gripped me intensely.

There were no signs of remorse for the human life that he charged with taking. This man's efforts were all geared to exist in a trash pile. He sacrificed a lot for a little. In his rage, he traded his future and landed under a mound of trash. There are many ways to forfeit our future, and there are a host of ways to exist in trash piles.

Naboth, the Jezreelite, had a vineyard located next to the king's palace. The vineyard was his patrimony. God had given it to his ancestors, and he refused to sell it, even to a king. Ahab sulked. Jezebel developed a scheme. She had Naboth framed for blasphemy. He was stoned to death, and they took his vineyard.

God's Vengeance: The word of the Lord came to Elijah at a time when Ahab and Jezebel felt secure in their cruelty, but God said, "In the place where dogs licked the blood of Naboth shall dogs lick thy blood, even thine." These judgments were leveled at both king and queen. Ahab went to battle. He tried to make King Jehoshaphat a decoy, but a soldier shot an arrow without aiming. It found Ahab. Some might call it coincidence. I call it providence. The king died. He was brought to Samaria. As they washed the chariot in which he died, "The dogs licked up his blood and they washed his armor," just as Elijah prophesied.

Fourteen years elapsed after the death of Ahab. Jezebel probably did not believe that God's word would come true and deliver her to a similar fate. For Jezebel, the circle was wide, but one day Jehu entered the gate. Jezebel spoke to him out of a window from which she was thrown by the eunuchs who stood at her side. Jehu went into the palace, ate, drank and sent word to bury Jezebel because she was the daughter of a king. Those who sought to carry out the orders "found no more of her than the skull, and the feet and the palms of her hands." The dogs had done their work. The prophecy had been fulfilled. People who do you wrong may well deserve more of your pity than your anger. As my grandmother would say, "If it doesn't come out in the washing, it will in the rinsing." Vengeance belongs to God!

- SEVEN -

HONEY ON THE GROUND

This chapter deals with blessings at the fingertips, which can come and go unnoticed. It also pleads for positive decision making regarding how we see what we have. Decision by indecision can be a dangerous pitfall. You can delay a decision until it is made for you by time or events. This approach trades away your God-given ability to choose the flavor of your days and the restfulness of your nights. God loves to bless. He does not have to be begged, only asked with a loving heart. God does not have to be chased down — He loves to bless. This is His nature. Blessing His people is as natural to God as breathing is to us.

When people harm you, you can become so absorbed in what they have done that you close your eyes to the blessings at your fingertips, living in the same house where you live, walking the same street that you walk, and working on the same job that you work. There is with our God-given freedom of choice a dual responsibility. Forgiving those who hurt us is not simply a good idea, it is a duty. It is a duty which provides for the doer both sight and insight. In the Book of 1 Samuel 14:24-27 a war was talking place:

> And the men of Israel were distressed that day: for Saul had adjured the people saying, cursed be the man that eateth any food until evening, that I may be avenged on mine enemies. So none of the people tasted any food. And all they of the land came to a wood; and there was honey upon the ground.

And when the people were come into the wood, behold, the honey dropped; but no man put his hand to his mouth for the people feared the oath. But Jonathan heard not when his father charged the people with the oath: wherefore he put forth the end of the rod that was in his hand, and dipped it in a honeycomb, and put his hand to his mouth; and his eyes were enlightened.

In this disconcerting setup, people were hit with hunger pains, while honey was on the ground. It was at their fingertips. It was within the reach of the most aged and weary among them. There were no trees to climb, no mountains to scale, and apparently no bees to combat. The blessing of honey paled in the light of a foolish oath made by Saul "to avenge" himself on his enemies. It was advantageous that Jonathan did not hear the oath, and therefore was not constrained by it. He reached. He dipped. He tasted and was renewed.

God always has some resource to renew us within our reach. When we forgive and commit the wrong doers to hands more efficient than ours, we are then able to do as Jonathan. Our hands become free to reach out had take hold of uncounted, and previously unrecognized, gifts dropped from above. I recall a saying that provides excellent advice, "Be kind, for everyone you meet is fighting some kind of a battle." You cannot be kind when you are consumed with bitterness. And if you can't be kind you cannot be free. I know of a man who owned a bulldog with a very mean spirit. When on one was around to attack, the dog would bite himself. The dog was tormented. Mean-spirited people do hurt others, but the damage mean-spirited people inflict in a self-injurious manner far outweighs the wounds they make in the lives of others.

Lessons from the Lesson of Ahithophel

2 Samuel 16—17. Ahithophel was a Gilonite. He was the grandfather of the beautiful Bathsheba, whom King David seduced, and later married. Ahithophel was the father of Eliam, a

captain in David's army. He probably had a great deal of respect for his king that was coupled only by his admiration for his son. Things changed. Tragedy struck. Arrogance is always distasteful, but is magnified when it comes from someone you respect. Pain is pain, and hurt is hurt. David's behavior grieved Ahithophel intensely. Bathsheba was surely the talk of the kingdom. To some, she was a victim; to others, she was a conspirator in a shameful murder plot, which included the death of her own husband. Regardless of what side people took, no side was advantageous to Bathsheba. Ahithophel credited David his granddaughter's sad status in the kingdom. It was a sad hour. But life did what it always does. It moved on, but Ahithophel was locked in a dark period. David and Bathsheba moved into the light (2 Sam. 12:24). The Bible informs us that the death of a child opened a brighter chapter in their lives "and David comforted Bathsheba his wife, and went in unto her, and lay with her: and she bare a son, and he called his name Solomon: and the LORD loved him."

Solomon grew up to become the wisest man of his day. He was the great-grandson of Ahithophel. However, there is no record of Ahithophel ever enjoying the precious God-given blessing of his unique great-grandson. Bathsheba became queen. Yet there is no place where we can see Ahithophel taking satisfaction in the new-found status of his granddaughter. He was locked in the past. Life had moved on, but he missed the joys the new days ushered in. David repented, but Ahithophel's heart was frozen.

The day of rebellion found a friend in Ahithophel. Absalom turned against his father David, and Ahithophel joined his conspiracy. Whether we live in the light or darkness, in the present or in the past, life always provides us with something to do. The rebellion of Absalom gave Ahithophel a chance to recover, repent or enlist. He chose the latter. He was so bitter, he counseled a son to "Go in unto thy father's concubines, which he hath left to keep the house; and all Israel shall hear that thou art abhorred of thy father; then shall the hands of all that are with thee be strong."

There is an old saying among African Americans that says, "Spite work won't work." God not only searches our behavior. He also examines our motives. God looks at what we do and why we do it with equal vision. The moral law of the universe works against those with impure motives. Jesus said in St. Luke 6:38, "Give, and it shall be given unto you, good measure, pressed down, and shaken together, and running over, shall men give into your bosom. For with the same measure that ye mete withal it shall be measured to you again." Our plans can work for or against us.

Ahithophel's advice was followed for a while, the day arrived when a more ambitious plan was promoted. Ahithophel wanted twelve thousand soldiers to pursue David and slay him. He was overruled. Hushai the Archite (2 Sam. 17:7) replaced him as counselor to Absalom. It was a brilliant suggestion. it was a great military strategy, but the counsel of Ahithophel was rejected. 2 Samuel 17:14 reveals a powerful statement.

And Absalom and all the men of Israel said, the counsel of Hushai the Archite is better than the counsel of Ahithophel, to the intent that the LORD might bring evil upon Absalom.

The things we work on only work out according to God's permission. Rejected and depressed Ahithophel leaves life on this side of the grave with this sad commentary in 2 Samuel 17:23:

And when Ahithophel saw that his counsel was not followed, he saddled is ass, and arose, and got him home to his house, to his city, and put his household in order, and hanged himself, and died, and was buried in the sepulcher of his father.

This man had a granddaughter for a queen, a genius for a great-grandson in Solomon, but bitterness drove him to hang himself. There was honey on the ground. He never saw it. He never tasted it. Life had moved on, but he was stationary.

When people do you wrong, it is not the end of your world. No matter what is taken from you, if you will think about it and let yourself see it, you will discover some honey on the ground.

Going on When Things Are Not Going Right

There is no such thing as the perfect time or the perfect place. I once knew a minister who always responded positively when questioned about the state of his life. When asked, "How are things going?" he responded, "Some things are great!" He was right! All things are never great, but some matters are great enough to keep you going. The right choices lead us in the right direction which will enable us to reach the right goals.

The cemetery at Tuskegee University in Tuskegee, Alabama, has a tombstone with a moving inscription. It reads "George Washington Carver — died in Tuskegee, Alabama, January 5, 1943. A life that stood out as a gospel of self-forgetful service. He could have added fortune to fame, but caring for neither, he found happiness and honor in being helpful to the world." Dr. Carver was born in slavery. He could have lived anywhere, yet he chose to live in the south. In spite of all the things that were not going right in the south at that time, Dr. Carver performed his work as a creative scientist. He was a man who lived in a sickly body. He was so prone to sickness as an infant, he was expected to die before reaching adolescence. He was stolen by night raiders and later swapped for a horse. In spite of his surroundings, he was so creative that he made a garage laundry more popular than a college president's office. Dr. Carver once stated that he prayed to God and asked for the secrets to the universe. He said God replied saying, "George, the secret to the universe it too big for you, but here is a peanut. Take it and work with it, and it will keep you busy."

Even when things are not going right for us, God gives us enough to keep us going. God gravitates enough opportunities our way to keep us busy. This life has a way of dealing us deuces instead of aces. But when our plans are interrupted, we should not erupt. When we are inconvenienced, we must avoid being incensed. Sometimes there are blessings even in our handicaps. There are blessings, opportunities, and unique gifts placed at our fingertips if we have the wisdom to reach.

Life at its best is balanced between good and bad, hard and soft, tears and laughter, and sweet and bitter experiences. The most beautiful flower gardens are products of both sunshine and rain. When the rain falls heavily, its purpose remains the same as it does when it is sprinkled gently. When the sunshine beats fiercely, its goal is the same as when its rays are a welcome sight ushering in the promises of a new day. The rain falls. The sun shines. There are varying degrees to a common purpose, yet the purpose greets every age unchanged. "How much is too much?" and "How little is too little?" are questions that often defy our finite minds and overwhelm our limited vision.

Along the shores of the ocean, the rocks are sharp in the quiet coves, but in the places where the waves beat against them, the rocks are always polished. God uses the heavy rainfalls and active waves of this life to polish us. There are in the facial lines of some elderly marks of stormy incidents. There is a kind of polished dignity that demands admiration and attention without having to say a word. You can find this look in the face of a seasoned statesperson in our nation's capital, and you can find it in the face of a grandparent in a public housing project. It is a picture of the victory of goodness over evil and courage over fear. I have seen the features, and so have you. They are priceless sights that are not easily won. Your difficult periods will service as a fitting room to dress you as a regal patriot. If you keep going, keep working, and keep learning, you will be amazed at the outcome.

You can experience the look of having the victory of good over evil. The reason is simple. There is a divine presence "to keep you at your best." I am thankful, that even as I have known the taste of bitter waters, there has been a presence to defend me from myself. The regal look is further undergirded by the strength of a humble spirit that knows who deserves the credit for the victory. It is "not I but Christ living in me" (Gal. 2:20). The regal spirit is never braggadocious. It knows who keeps it at its best. The person who receives a gift has nothing to be boastful about. The gift says more about the giver than it does about the person who simply accepts it.

- Eight -

You Must Forgive For Your Own Well Being

A cup filled with sand cannot hold a cup filled with water. You cannot think two thoughts at the same time. You cannot kick and pull at the same time. You cannot forgive and hate. It is always in our personal best interest to forgive and not house hostility. I did not say forget. All knowledge from our past can make us wise. When we forgive what has gone on before, we can much more accurately forecast the events to come. Søren Kierkegaard once said, "Life must be lived forwards; but it can only be understood backwards." Life will not make any sense unless yesterday's experiences have something to do with today's living. It is foolish to face each day as if you have just fallen off "a turnip truck" and walked into town for the first time. The knowledge that fire burned us yesterday should be sufficient information to keeps us from testing to see if it will burn us today. I am not advocating forgetfulness. As a matter of fact, I am telling you that in some cases, with some people, it is imprudent to forget. But while it is unwise to forget, it is equally unwise not to forgive. Forgiving and forgetting are not the same thing. Forgetting is a matter of the head — forgiving is a matter of the heart. Proverbs 4:23 says, "Keep thy heart with all diligence; for out of it are the issues of life."

When you forgive a person for an act, the act no longer dominates your image of the person. Prior to forgiveness, whenever you think of the person, the act monopolizes your image of the person. You reduce that person to your pain and you prolong your hurt. God wants you to be happy and free. God wants you to know the release that comes when you drop the weight you are carrying.

Freedom

Sometimes what we think is virtuous is not close to being appropriate. In Matthew 18:1-35, we find an emphasis that speaks to all of our needs. What is popular and what is powerful is often conflictual. During the time of our Lord, the prevalent teaching on forgiveness limited it to three times. Peter probably expected praise when he raised the number to seven times. It is interesting to note the way Peter coined the question. Peter asked Jesus, "How often shall I forgive my brother who sins against me? Till seven times?" Jesus responded by saying, "Until seventy times seven," which is 490 times. It would be easier to forgive than to keep count. Jesus illustrated this great truth by sharing a parable.

A man was in debt. In the parable a servant owed his king. It was no small debt. The Bible says the man owed 10,000 talents. This amount of money could be calculated at the amount of ten million dollars. The repayment was beyond the man's ability. He could not work it out. He could not borrow it. He was in deep, far over his head. This servant was doomed except for the mercy of the king. The king forgave him. The man was not deserving, but he had one good thing going for himself. He had a good master. The man was not lucky. He was blessed to have been in debt to a master who was merciful enough to write off his debt.

This, of course, is a portrait of the heavenly king in whose debt we each fall. We have in our own way, through our own errors, faults, mistakes, habits, weaknesses, and sins (we have fallen short of what God requires). There is, however, good news. God will forgive. He is rich in mercy. We must seek Him, be honest with Him, and humble ourselves before Him. He will forgive all our sins. Only God is big enough to do it, and only God desires to do it for any and for all. Instead of being cast into the prisons as he deserved, the servant was forgiven, set free, and given another chance to make the most of his life. He who wronged his king was set free.

A Man Who Had Been Forgiven Refused to Forgive Another for a Lesser Debt

The servant who was forgiven of his debt went from his king's presence to another man who in turn, owed him one 100 pence (about $1,600). Once out of the king's presence, the servant became hard-hearted, selfish, and forgetful. The man who owed him money begged for patience. He caught him by the throat, refused his plea, and had him thrown in jail. The man forgot his own guilt, his own dangerous debt, and threw a man in prison whose debt was small in comparison to his own. What he wanted for himself, he refused to give to another. The master, when he heard, was furious. He had his servant seized and cast into prison. There is no place in the parable which even suggests that the man who owed the lesser debt was ever set free.

My friends, you can imprison good people who wrong you by failing to forgive them. Some marriages are time bombs, simply because one partner is shackled by the other's unforgiveness. The morality of the issue should have forced the forgiven man to forgive his brother. We may not have the same faults, but we do have faults. And in the economy of God, sin is not placed on a scale from one to ten and rated. Sin is sin! Wrong is wrong! A mistake is a mistake! A debt is a debt! We who have been forgiven must "live and let live."

A. *The Model Prayer* — Matthew 6:12-15: "And forgive us our debts, as we forgive our debtors. And lead us not into temptation, but deliver us from evil: For thine is the kingdom, and the power, and the glory, forever. Amen. For if ye forgive men their trespasses, your heavenly Father will also forgive you: but if ye forgive not men their trespasses, neither will your Father forgive your trespasses."

B. *Spiritual Cleansing.* The ermine is a weasel with a soft white fur. The position, rank and functions of a judge, whose state robe, in European countries, is trimmed in ermine as an emblem of honor and purity. During the Middle Ages, people used the ermine to keep strangers away. It was stationed at the entry. The grounds were grassless. The ermine would fight to the death to stay on the slab at the entry rather than be cast into the dust or mud. The ermine's white coat was its badge of purity. It would rather die than have it stained. The ermine was committed to keeping its coat clean. The Bible teaches us that unforgiven sin pollutes us. It destroys fellowship and will ruin relationships with friends and families. James tells us of a way that we can experience spiritual cleansing.

> And the prayer of faith shall save the sick, and the Lord shall raise him up; and if he has committed sins, they shall be forgiven him. Confess your faults one to another, and pray one for another, that ye may be healed. The effectual fervent prayer of a righteous man availeth much (James 5:15-16).

The Unforgiving Man Lost His Freedom

It was not long before the deeds of the unforgiving man reached the ears of his master. The master was angry. When the man came before him in debt he did not call him wicked, but when the master heard of his hard hearted mistreatment of his debtor he said, "O thou wicked servant." His mean-spirited treatment canceled out his own forgiveness. His master had rescued him earlier, but his own unmercifulness put him back into prison. The worst prison in the world is the prison of an unrepentant and unforgiving heart. An unforgiving heart will keep a father or mother from enjoying their children. A man or woman can be so imprisoned by a broken relationship that they park their emotional lives in a no-parking zone, which keeps them out of the reach of a brighter and better life. Sometimes the greatest gifts come by way of our unanswered prayers. The thing we want the most is usually what we need the least. An unnamed poet best described the sentiment:

> *I asked for strength that I might achieve;*
> *He made me weak that I might obey.*
> *I asked for health that I might do greater things;*
> *I was given grace that I might do better things.*
> *I asked for riches that I might be happy;*
> *I was given poverty that I might be wise.*
> *I asked for power that I might have the praise of men;*
> *I was given weakness that I might feel the need of God.*
> *I asked for all things that I might enjoy life;*
> *I was given life that I might enjoy all things.*
> *I received nothing that I asked for.*
> *All that I hoped for,*
> *My prayer was answered.*

Seeing Heaven Open Up

When you forgive, your vision into spiritual realities improves. The person who has no vision is one who is cheated. This is true because that kind of person only sees a small part of reality. Electricity was just as real in the days of the Bible as it is today. But it was not until Thomas Edison caught a vision of the unseen, that a curse was turned into a blessing.

What we are determines what we see. A vulture can fly over a landscape painted by thousands of beautiful flowers. He might look upon roses, marigolds, and multicolored impatients without every seeing a flower, yet he will see a decayed or dying animal even if it is partly covered by weeds and woods. He should not be blamed because he sees what he sees because of what he is. A cold and unforgiving heart can blind us to a world of beautiful sights. A cold heart will have us sighing when we ought to be singing. It will keep us from seeing beauty where beauty exists. The Book of Acts shares a profound revelation. The insight escalates out of the stoning of Stephen (read Acts 7:54-60)

Few of us will know the level of outrage which escalated into killing Stephen. While many of you, drawn to this book, could write your own story, many can empathize with Stephen. There are some things you just do not expect from some people. The religious rulers clenched their fists, gnashed their teeth, and spewed out a kind of hatred that came straight from hell. Stephen had courted death, it arrived by the hands of religious men. Their faces were flushed with a pulsating anger, but he did not see that. Being a forgiving man, Stephen was able to see beyond force and fury. His own words were, "I see the heavens opened, and the Son of man standing at the right hand of God." A view of heaven opened up and enabled Stephen to forgive his enemies as they stoned him. One blessing drove another. Forgiveness begets forgiveness. When you realize you are forgiven, you will forgive.

The scenery around Stephen was saturated with violence, but in the midst of it all, he caught a vision that brought him that unspeakable peace that surpasseth all human understanding. Heedless of the fleeting stones that crushed his body, Stephen fell asleep only to awaken to a better life.

- NINE -

GOOD OUT OF EVIL

In his mercy, God providentially takes an evil act and wrings from it timeless blessing. At creation God spoke to the darkness and said, "Let there be light" because He saw light hiding under the cover of darkness. As one writer has said, "God sees what He says and He says what He sees." If God speaks to the darkness and says, "Let there be light," it is because He sees light in the darkness. We must remember that God is still doing what He did and saying what He said and sometimes He upsets in order to set up. Genesis 27:41-46 reveals how Jacob had to flee to Haran to escape the wrath of his brother Esau because of what he had done.

Every behavior has a cost. Sometimes we cannot see it, feel it, or measure it, but there seems to be a law written into the very fabric of the universe extracting a price from us for our actions. Jacob cheated his brother and deceived his father. His brother Esau's anger sent him packing. Things were a mess. He lost his home. His own brother hated him. His mother could not protect him, and his dreams seemed to turn to ashes in his hands. But God sees around the corner far better than we can see gazing in a straight line. The goodness of God overruled the badness of Jacob. God took his mess and led him to Haran. There in Haran, he found wealth, love, family, and fathered the twelve tribes of Israel (Gen. 28 — 31). Jacob did not deserve it, and he certainly could not have orchestrated it; but God, in His goodness, who is rich in His mercy, performed it. God took Laban's broken promise, Jacob's knowledge of livestock and some poetic justice and mixed that which seemed to be unrelated into a perfect recipe for blessing. Only God is wise enough to take an unwanted bride from an unwanted trip through an unwanted contract and create and answer to prayer!

As finite beings, we are often caught in the flow of a mysterious current. We cannot determine the speed or direction of our journey but if we seek divine assistance and approval, God will make the destination well worth any inconveniences or hardships. Without the power of God, we fail in our strength, but with His fatherly concern we are called to tread no wine press alone. As our Father, God is our Producer, Provider, and Protector. As our Producer, He creates, as our Provider, He constructs. As our Protector, He controls. Right can come out of wrong because God can find it, refine it, and revive it if we will only refer it to Him. At Bethel, Jacob found out that while he could not bless himself there was a God who was able.

If You Want to Be Blessed, You've Got to Make a Vow

Good comes from evil as a result of spiritual blessedness. This is not some peripheral gift that is as accessible to lightweights in the spirit as it is to those who have deepened their roots. God sends material blessings upon everybody, but the gifts of the spirit only come to those who are spirit-led. God's best gifts are spiritual because everything that is material is constrained by time, and those things that are limited by time eventually wear out. Genesis 28:20-22 states:

> And Jacob vowed a vow, saying, if God will be with me, and will keep me in this way that I go, and will give me bread to eat, and raiment to put on, so that I come gain to my father's house in peace; then shall the Lord be my God: And this stone, which I have set for a pillar, shall be God's house: and of all that thou shalt give me I will surely give the tenth unto thee.

When we get serious enough to commit ourselves to God, we are preparing ourselves for spiritual blessings. I am not referring here to lip service or to what I call "sick bed" desperation. When some people are in trouble or sick, they make all kinds of promises that they feel will better their condition. The vow that Jacob makes here is much deeper. It is not a trick hurled by a tricky man but a prayer prayed by a sinner who discovered the answer for his sins. A great missionary, Lott Carey, once said, "Do great things for God and expect great things from God." Jacob reached a point where he sees God for who He is and for what He can do. This realization made a great impact on him. Up to this point, we only see Jacob taking, but a knowledge of God's true causes him to give.

If you want to be happy and win, even when it looks like you are losing, deal with God from your giving self. Once we confront God with our giving self, we are set free to live in this world as a contributor rather than just a consumer.

When people do you wrong they can affect your getting self, but only you and God determine your giving self. You can always give. You can be confined to a sick room and give inspiration to others by the way you bear your sickness. You can share a word, say a prayer, send a card, pick up a nail, or perform a hundred other helping deeds. Even a full glass of water can take one more drop. Every feathered nest has a thorn in it. Our world is a needy world, and when you confront it from a viewpoint of giving rather than getting, you will be amazed at the rate in which your usefulness quotient will be raised. I think that it is important for each of us to remember that our influence can survive our physical bodies.

A small girl was at a vacation resort with her parents. The child sat in a chair, fanning herself with a beautiful silk fan. A man approached her and asked the child if he could borrow her fan overnight. The child refused and ran off to her parents. After some investigation the parents discovered that the man who wanted to borrow the fan was a famous artist and wanted to paint a picture of the fan. The fan cost less than five dollars but a painting of this five-dollar fan by that famous artist would have been valued above five thousand dollars. The artist knew what he could do, but he did not wrestle the fan away from the child. However, if she had given it to him he could have made it more valuable.

We can put our lives into the hands of powers that will devalue them or we can trust and commend ourselves into heavenly hands that will plant heavenly treasures into earthen vessels. This comes not by chance but by choice. Without a doubt, there is implanted in the human soul a desire for fellowship. Life is absolutely lonely without it. Happiness is always multiplied when it is shared, and trouble is always lightened when it is divided.

God makes the first move of love. He starts the journey. He makes the first contact. He speaks the first word. He opens the first gate. But we have to respond. If we fail to respond, we will be left with the material blessings, but will close the door to the deeper spiritual blessings. Good can come out of evil. Right can come out of wrong, but only with God's help. There is no such things as an independent ship upon life's high seas. We all look ahead every once in a while, for tomorrow's sunrise is really tinted in the sunset colors from today. The star that pins the curtains of the nightfall whispers to us of a coming morning, when those same curtains shall be drawn apart. We who are wise scan our horizon because we know that tomorrow will come as surely as today is already here.

And there is no tomorrow that sets us free from the need of a real friend. Henry Ford once said, "My best friend is he who brings out the best in me." A word from an acquaintance carries little weight, but a word from a real friend is weighty. Real friendship always shines brighter in trouble because trouble. Trouble is to friendship what acid is to gold. Trouble does not intimidate godly friendship. It only reveals it. God sees in the dark, and He sees in our troubles something you and I cannot envision. The story goes that a sculptor whose touch seemed endowed with magic was questioned by a child. When pressed for his secret, he simply replied, "An angel was in the marble. I only cut away the stone from around it and let it go free." God sees angels hidden inside many of the blocks that confront us. He sees, and He sets free. No one can see what God sees.

We all make the mistake of elevating false friends to God-like status, and we end up paying for it. Some of them talk us out of blessings, and some lead us into traps. Be careful making vows. Be selective as to whose voice you heed, even among your friends. Just because you like someone and that person likes you does not mean that person is trustworthy. Jacob made a vow to God. God blessed him and brought him because Jacob delivered himself into hands that were strong enough to hold. Before Jesus died upon the ross he said, "Father into thy hands I commend my Spirit." The word *commend* in the Greek text comes from the Greek word *paratithemai*. The word means "to deliver something, to take up and carry it from one place to another." When we deliver ourselves, our gifts, our failures, our limitation, our very all into the hands of this divine Friend who is also our Father, we will be blessed. Isn't it great to have a Father who is a friend and who loves, forgives, protects, and remains when all others walk out!

As our Father, God requires things from us. If God simply worked on our behalf without requiring something from us, we would soon develop an entitlement mentality. There are many things wrong with an entitlement mentality, of which ingratitude and selfishness are the two most noticeable.

God at Work in Us

God not only wants to work for us, He wants to work in us, to develop us into beings that are willing to be used. We are more than creatures of the moment. We are in the world but not of the world. At our best, we live a life that is too big to put in a casket and too powerful to lock in a grave. True character is not born of blood. People are not good or bad because of their ancestry. Each person has to pay his own rent. God does not seek to simply govern us; He seeks to reside within us in order to mature us, enrich us, and increase our usefulness. It is never enough to keep a child off the street; a successful parent makes the child want to stay off the street. The key is not working from the outside in, but from the inside out. It is not easy. It takes time. It is costly, but it is more important than money. History is replete with examples that illustrate this point.

Both France and England were threatened by revolution. The same forces were boiling in England and France. France had a standing army and a Bourbon king. France exploded, and the streets ran crimson in blood. England did not have a strong military, but it had an educational movement, a Protestant church, and the Wesleyan movement. These internal factors blessed the nation and held off bloodshed.

Many people have done more with less while others keep doing less with more. The God factor continues to be the mission reality. John 1:10-13 states:

> He was in the world, and the world was made by Him, and the world knew Him not. He came unto His own, and His own received Him not. But as many as received Him, to them gave He power to become the sons of God, even to them that believe on His name: which were born, not of blood, nor of the will of the flesh, nor of the will of man, but of God.

Neither will power, inheritance, culture, government, or education brood greatness of character. It is the God factor. It is the living, abiding, divinely reinforced presence of the Almighty working inside that correctly impacts on the outside. You cannot hang fruit on a tree and call the tree fruitful anymore than you can paint a smile on a child and call it self-esteem. There are some things that are inside jobs, and if they are not done from the inside, they are not done at all.

God Works in Single Family Households

We are all saddened by the number of single family households, but in our sadness we are forgetting a great truth. It is not the number of parents, but it is the kind of parent a child has that will make the difference. We all know of many people who have turned out quite well as products of single family households. It is a blessing for a child to have both parents, but children without both parents are not cursed.

Hagar

Genesis 1:9-21

And Sarah saw the son of Hagar the Egyptian, which she had born unto Abraham, mocking. Wherefore she said unto Abraham, cast out this bondwoman and her son: for the son of this bondwoman shall not be heir with my son, even with Isaac. And the thing was very grievous in Abraham's sight because of his son. And God said unto Abraham, let it not be grievous in thy sight because of the lad, and because of thy bondwoman; in all that Sarah halt said unto thee, hearken unto her voice; for in Isaac shall thy seed be called. And also of the son of the bondwoman will I make a nation, because he is thy seed. And Abraham rose up early in the morning, and took bread, and a bottle of water, and gave it unto Hagar, putting it on her shoulder, and the child, and sent her away: and she departed, and wandered in the wilderness of Beersheba. And the water was spent in the bottle, and she cast the child under one of the shrubs. And she went, and sat her down over against him a good way off as it were a bow shot: For she said, let me not see the death of the child. And she sat over against him, and lift up her voice, and wept. And God heard the voice of the lad; and the angel of God called to Hagar out of heaven, and said unto her, what aileth thee, Hagar? Fear not; for God hath heart the voice of the lad where he is. Arise, lift up the lad, and hold him in thine hand; for I will make him a great nation. And God opened her eyes, and she saw a well of water, and she went, and filled the bottle with water, and gave the lad drink. And God was with the lad; and he grew, and dwelt in the wilderness, and became an archer. And he dwelt in the wilderness of Paran: and his mother took him a wife out of the land of Egypt. (Genesis 1:9-21)

Hagar knew what it meant to be wronged. She knew what it meant to be a single female parent in a world where a woman's status was more often than not determined by the men in her life. She was a slave out of her native land. She had been plucked from the soil of her people, ultimately planted into the bed of Abraham, then cast out into the desert with a son, some bread, a bottle of water, and promises for future provisions.

There were no social service agencies advocating aid to dependent children. She did not move into a low-income apartment, she was sent away into a desert, with no income. Hagar was a victim of a normal system in her day, yet God brought good out of evil. If God cold save, bless, and promote in this perilous scenario, He will surely do no less today. A chance with God is always superior to a chance with things.

Being cast out, Hagar lost her chance for a lot of good things, such as the comfort, security, and protection of the tents of Abraham. However, she landed in a place that gave her a better chance at God. Packed up and sent off with nothing but a piece of bread and a bottle of water, she ran into God, and God introduced Himself, revealed His heart, and demonstrated His power.

God Was Concerned

Her water ran out. Hagar was bereft of hope, and she laid her son under the shade of a shrub, lifted up her voice, and wept. God is moved by our tears. People might rejoice in them, but God is affected by our tears. God said to Hezekiah through the prophet Isaiah, "I have seen thy tears: behold, I will heal thee" (2 Kings 20:5).

God asked, "What aileth thee, Hagar?" God knew that her condition was severe. He asked her the question only to make her aware that He knew something was wrong. God was making her aware of the fact that He sees and cares. God is a God of concern. When others change their telephone numbers, leaves their answering machines on, or change their residence, God cares! God has the time to care. He asked, "What aileth thee, Hagar?" God was saying, "Whatever it is, bring it to me, and I will help you. You have given up, but I have not. You are hopeless, but I am the God of hope. You are at the end of your strength, but I am not at the end of mine. However tragic your situation may be, though there is nothing else that you can do, there is always something else that I can do. Remember that man's extremity is God's opportunity. I know. I am interested. I am able. Therefore, tell me your story. Put your case in my hands."

Sarah had wronged her. Abraham had deserted her, but God was still on the throne. He is the source of strength, power, and endurance that will make demons flee, devils weep, and enemies shake their heads in disbelief. God is on the throne. He sees. He hears. He works. He moves. He watches. He knows. He cares and He is always asking, "What aileth thee?"

What is wrong with you? God speaks to every deserted soul abandoned by flesh and blood and says, "I am standing by!"

God said to Hagar, "Arise, lift up the lad, and hold him in thy hand." Hagar had given up. She had left her son under a shrub. Hard times are not hopeless times. Nothing is over until God decrees that the end has come. Nobody is finished and nothing is resolved until it meets divine approval. Hagar made a big mistake and was wrong. She thought that death had come, but God had other plans and told her that His plans overruled her depression and exceeded her limits. God told here to go back and pick up the lad and hold him in her hands. God is not intimidated because one parent is gone, and one is left. God is not limited by numbers nor frustrated by earth-born predictions or human made barriers. God said to Hagar, "Lift up the lad and hold him in thy hands." He was telling her not to take her hands off him and never to act like it is over until I say so.

God opened her eyes, and she saw a well of water. God had heard the cry of her child and said, "Fear not." The fear is the father of failure. When we learn to fear God, we drop the fears of living in a world that is created and maintained by God. Our failures are often pre-existent in our fears. God spoke to Hagar and said, "Fear not. You are in the desert. Your case is serious, but you are not alone. Sarah flexed her muscles and Abraham sent you off. but that was yesterday. Today is a new day. Live it. Seize it. Rejoice in it."

With the help of God every day carries with it something good. God opened the eyes of Hagar, and she saw a well. I do not believe that the well was dropped from heaven. It had been there all along, but she could not see it until God spoke. When we hear and heed the voice of God, we see things through discerning eyes and our vision always improves. God met her present need by improving her vision. He healed her future fears by simply "being with the lad." The fact God was with Ishmael caused him to grow, glow, and prosper. It worked that way in a desert long ago, and it can work that way in any place, from bucolic settings where people make their living from the soil to the affluent townhouses where crowds operate in the concrete jungles that we call cities.

Jephthah

Now Jephthah the Gileadite was a mighty man of valor, and he was the son of an harlot: and Gilead begot jephthah. And Gilead's wife bore him sons; and his wife's sons grew up, and they thrust our Jephthah, and said unto him, thou shalt not inherit in our father's house; for thou art the son of a strange woman. Then Jephthah fled from his brethren, and dwelt in the land of Tob: and there were gathered vain men to jephthah, and went out with him. And it came to pass in process of time, that the children of Ammon made ware against Israel, the elders of Gilead went to fetch jephthah out of the land of Tob: and they said unto Jephthah, come, and be our captain, that we may fight with the children of Ammon. And Jephthah said unto the elders of Gilead, did not ye hate me, and expel me out of my father's house? And why are ye come unto me now when ye are in distress? And the elders of Gilead said unto jephthah, therefore we turn again to thee now, that thou mayest go with us, and fight against the children of Ammon, and be our head over all the inhabitants of Gilead. And Jephthah said unto the elders of Gilead, if ye bring me home again to fight against the children of Ammon, and the Lord deliver them before me, shall I be your head? And the elders of Gilead said unto Jephthah, the Lord be witness between us, if we do not so according to thy words. Then Jephthah went with the elders of Gilead, and the people made him head and captain over them: and Jephthah uttered all his words before the Lord in Mizpah. (Judges 11:1-11)

Jephthah was the son of a harlot. His mother was a professional outcast. His father was married to both a woman who never accepted him and a tradition that clearly condemned him. Jephthah knew what it felt like to be considered unclean, unwelcome, and undervalued. He was not the blame for his birth, but he was treated as if he were responsible for it. It is not clear how his father, whose name was Gilead, felt about his mother, but he recognized Jephthah as his son. He brought him into his home, but Jephthah was never accepted as a brother. The Bible tells us that Gilead provided for him during his lifetime.

The Law, however, excluded him. Deuteronomy 23:2-3 says, "A bastard shall not enter into the congregation of the Lord; even to his tenth generation shall he not enter into the congregation of the Lord. An Ammonite or a Moabite shall not enter into the congregation of the Lord; even to the tenth generation shall they not enter into the congregation of the Lord forever." Religion was against him, culture was against him, and when his father died, his brothers openly spoke against him saying to Jephthah, "Thou are son of a strange woman." They cast him out, he had no unemployment resources, no free lunches, no sympathetic favors from tribal giants or kind hearted gestures from a compassionate priesthood. He who had been put down was put out with no inheritance. He suffered greatly, and he was branded with a shame that really did not belong to him. Jephthah was a victim who was blamed for his father's sin and his mother's profession. There were many factors that affected him that he had no control over, but there was one decision that he made that allowed God to go to work in him. When they threw him out, Jephthah turned his face not only toward the land of Tob, but also toward God.

At the excavation of the ancient city of Pompeii, the body of a woman was found. The city was destroyed by the fires from Vesuvius. The woman's body had been embalmed by the ashes. Her feet were turned toward the gate of the city but her face was turned backward. She had turned her face around. She was headed, feet first, in the right direction, but she turned her head around and reached for a bag of pearls. She might have dropped them or she might have seen someone else drop them. She was in a crisis. Death was hard on her track, but instead of running to safety, she turned her head, reached for the pearls, and died reaching. It was not the eruption of Vesuvius, but it was her unwillingness to travel in the right direction that sealed her doom.

Jephthah turned in the direction of God. He was cut off, but not cut out, even though his brothers cast him out. God intervened, time brought change. The same people who scorned him had to look up one day and honor him as their leader. It was not luck. It was not fate. Jephthah viewed his change in status as divinely ordered. He was right. Nobody has to give up when God is given a chance. Nobody at the bottom has to be confined to the bottom when God is allowed to work. When we do our duty where we are with what we have, God gives the increase. God brought good out of evil. A reject became a leader. Having turned in the direction of God, Jephthah developed the wisdom of an old Irish toast which says, "May you have the hindsight to know where you've been, the foresight to know where you're going, and the insight to know when you're going too far." This life is one where we have to strike balances, and it is often necessary for us to have revelation as opposed to simple information. Knowledge can come from around but wisdom comes from above. "If any of you lack wisdom, let him ask of God, that giveth to all men liberally, and upbraideth not; and it shall be given him" (James 1:5).

Jabez

> And Jabez was more honorable than his brethren: and his mother called his name Jabez, saying, because I bare him with sorrow. And Jabez called on the God of israel, saying, Oh that thou wouldest bless me indeed, and enlarge my coast, and that thine hand might be with me, and that thou wouldest keep me from evil, that it may not grieve me! And God granted him that which he requested. (1 Chronicles 4:9-10)

What we know about Jabez is revealed in these two verses. It is not unreasonable to view him as a product of a single-family household. We are not given the specific reasons that moved his mother to give him a name which means "sorrowful." However, we are informed that she bore him in great sorrow. The fact that the mother named Jabez clearly indicates that his father died before he was born. In that male-dominated culture, mothers did not name their children. The naming of a child was the privilege of the father. His mother named him sorrowful either because she feared for his chances of enjoying a successful future or because she was pained at his birth which revealed some kind of handicap that would make his life miserable.

In that culture a name meant more than it does today. Some parents invent names because of the sound, with no thought of substance. Ours is a world where the question "What is the baby's name?" is seldom followed up by the question, "What does the name mean?' This was not the case with Jabez. In his day, a name was descriptive of the person who received the name. A name, at that hour in history, was taken as a symbol of character. Great care and thought was given to the naming of a child, and in that setting, something somewhere was so ominous that "his mother called his name Jabez saying because I bare him with great sorrow."

We often discuss the impact of parental messages in the development of the internal dialogue that shapes self-esteem. We hear countless arguments about "self-fulfilling prophecies." But here is a man who grew up with the disability of a motherly name tag hanging around his neck. We are not told that his mother gave weird names to his brothers, yet the history of that family is summed up in the words which say, "Jabez was more honorable than his brethren." He had many things going against him, but he purposed in his heart to be honorable, and in his family, there was no equal.

What then do you do when your own mother names you Jabez? How do you react when you are standing at the starting gate, and the other runners have taken off at full speed and are well on their way down the track? How do you overcome when a bad day at somebody else's house is better than a good day in your own home? What do you do when you play by a given set of rules in the outfield, giving everybody at bat three strikes before they are out, but when your turn to hit comes around, the strike zone is widened, the number of allowed strikes is reduced, and the fence is moved back? How do you keep job hunting when your interviews are meaningless because the decision has already been made to exclude you? How do you keep going when you make the same mistake that others make, but yours is treated more severely? How do you react when others have the same flaws as you, but their flaws are overlooked altogether while yours are penalized and scrutinized? Is there any formula for victory in a world that is saturated with, "you won't" and "you don't"? Is it possible to have any "bootstraps" to pull up when you are all on your own?

In a setting where you are constantly confronted with too this or too that, is it possible to strike something that is just right? In the life of Jabez, there are answers to these questions and countless others. He did not whine, he did not quit. The outlook was horrible, but the up look changed everything. Jabez called on the Lord. God not only has the power to bless, but God always has the time to bless. If we take our case to the right source, we can get the right relief.

There is a cotton mill factory where there are posters on the walls in full view of all the employees. The posters contains a simple message which says, "If your threads get tangled, send for the foreman." A young woman started to work in that factory after having searched for jobs in vain. She was excited, industrious, and conscientious. She worked hard and demonstrated all the attributes of a sound work ethic, but one day her threads got tangled. She did not want to seem inept so she tried to untangle the threads by herself. She made a mess! The harder she tried to untangle the threads the worse the problem got. Finally, she sent for the foreman. When he got there he looked at the problem and asked, "Have you been trying to fix this problem by yourself?" She answered in the affirmative. He reminded her of the posters and asked, "Why didn't you send for me?" She answered by saying, "I was trying to fix it. I did my best." The foreman corrected her by saying, "You did not do your best. You tried to fix the problem, you stayed on task. You stood by your machine. You didn't clock out early and go home, but you did not do your best. You must never forget that doing your best means that you follow directions." We never do our best when the threads of living get tangled until we send for the divine Foreman. When He arrives, He can easily do what we cannot. His power is supernatural. His knowledge is supernatural. His resources are from a supernatural storehouse, and His tools work with a supernatural efficiency because nothing is too hard for God.

Jabez asked God to bless him. He asked that God's hand would be upon him. He reached for God's hand, and he saw himself as a glove that had no life apart from the divine hand. He prayed that God would keep him from evil. This is not a request for freedom from toil. He asked to be kept from evil.

In the world in which we live, there are some people who are evildoers. They will do evil things to us. They will say evil things about us. They will develop evil traps to harm us. When Jabez prayed that God would keep him from evil, he was not asking for exemption from battle. He was praying the same kind of prayer Jesus prayed when He said, "I pray not that thou shouldest take them out of the world, but that thou shouldest keep them from evil." Jabez prayed, "that thou wouldest keep me from evil, that it may not grieve me." He was asking God to keep the reins, set the limits, draw a fixed line, mark out a definite boundary, and establish an unmoveable marker on what evil could do and where it could go.

Evil, unchecked, is dangerous beyond our finite imagination. The depraved mind and heart that is away from God can sink to levels that are far too low for us to measure. When people bomb buildings in peaceful places, we see the ugliness and destructiveness of evil.

Jabez asked God to enlarge his coast. He was praying for a big life. He did not want to be narrow, selfish, or circumscribed. This man wanted to wake up every day expecting to cover new ground. He did not wish for an easy life. He wanted to get it on, day after day, always learning, always climbing, always reaching, and always discovering something that would make his pulse quicken and send his heart racing.

God wants no less for you and me. People will do you wrong. Some will try to stop you, but God is still in the work of enlarging coasts. No, you cannot make chicken salad out of chicken feathers, but you can make a pretty comfortable pillow to rest on while you give God a chance to enlarge your coast. Do what you can with what you have, and God will work in you to do what you cannot if you will only give Him a chance.

You have not done your best until you send for Him. He knows what He makes and what He makes, He knows how to maintain. Every time I think about this, I get excited and feel a bit like the old farmer who shouted too much for some of the folks in his home church. They sent a committee to him in order to discuss curbing his shouting proclivity. When the delegation arrived, they found him plowing in the fields. They did not mince words. They stated their purposes and made their request. The old farmer responded by giving them a long litany of God's favors to him. He had been sick. God healed him. He had been isolated. God gave him a family. He had been poor. God blessed him with a home. He had been a sharecropper. God gave him his own farm. He had been lost. God saved his soul. Tears began to well up in his eyes as he talked, and he turned to a member of the delegation and said, "Y'all excuse me, but if someone will hold my mule, I'll shout right here."

God will enlarge your coast! God will expand your world. God will stretch your experiences into places that you never knew existed, and that is worth getting somebody to hold your mule while you shout about it for a while. His mother called his name Jabez, but God enlarged his coasts and he "was more honorable than his brethren."

God is able to bring good out of conditions that seem to bear no good. It is a fact that God is good all of the time, and even when the thunder rolls and the lightning flashes, God is busy blessing His world. Every time the lightning flashes, God is meeting our needs. We, as human beings, need nitrogen for our bodies. Nitrogen abounds in the atmosphere, but we cannot inhale it and absorb it through our lungs. But the God who made us knows us, and He is thoughtful of our needs. God send a charge of lightning. The lightning separates the nitrogen from the atmosphere. Then God drops some rain to wash it down from above. We still cannot absorb it but God prepares a little bacteria that transforms the nitrate into a nitrite so that a plant can absorb it. We eat the plant or an animal comes by and eats the plant. Then we eat the animal that ate the plant that absorbed the nitrate that used to be a nitrate that God cut loose with a bolt of lightning in the first place! (Hold my mule!) So the next time you see a flash of lightning, say a prayer of thanksgiving. The same God who sends the lightning can be sent for. If we call, He will come. If we reach out, He will reach in. If we look out and things look bad, look up and the uplook will change everything.

When people do you wrong, be careful where you take your grievance. If you take it in and chew on it, it can choke you. If you digest it and harbor it, it can destroy you. If you place it in the wrong hands, it can depress you; but if you take your cast to the right source, good can come out of evil, blessings from burdens, and promotions from terminations. The end of one thing with God's help, is often the beginning of a better thing. Dag Hammarskjold, former secretary of the United Nations, once said, "A man at war with himself will be at war with everyone else." When we take our grievances to God, we avoid making ourselves an enemy that must do internal battle with ourselves and eternal warfare with Him. People who stay at war with others do so because they are at war with themselves. There are many things that we cannot stop people from doing, but we can prevent them from starting a war within us. As we give God our grievances, He gives us His comfort, even if He does not change our condition.

The word *comfort* in the Greek form. comes from the world *parakleo* which means "to come beside." Jabez called on the Lord and the Lord "came beside" him. It is no great surprise that with divine companionship he became more honorable than his brethren.

A very wise man was insulted one day by a youthful critic. The wise man responded to the verbal barbs by asking the youth a question. He said, "Son, if someone declined to accept a present, to whom would it belong?" The young man paused, thought about it and said, "To him who offered it." The wise man replied, "And so, I decline to accept your abuse." Jabez was named "Sorrowful," but he declined to accept either the limitation or the prophecy of his name. By grace we can respond in the same way; we can have the strength to be steadfast. Hebrews 11:27 says of Moses, "He endured, as seeing Him who is invisible." It was the God factor that created a deep and constant force from within with which Moses, Jabez, and others met the strange vicissitudes of this life. Try any other key to their endurance and to their lives and you will find that it will not open. None of us can endure in any other way. We need the spiritual and the spiritual is what Gods pleads with us to accept.

- TEN -

THE POWER OF PRAYER

Many years ago, I read a statement which said, "Prayer can do anything that God can do." I was taken. I thought about it, brooded over it, and have adopted that belief system with untold and unmeasured success. For me, prayer is not some emergency spare tire to get me from a crisis to a better location. It has become a way of life that is as natural as breathing. Prayer is, of course, a Christian duty, but it is far more. To be able to pray is one of the highest privileges that the Divine has turned our feeble way. When you pray right, you are given access to the source of power that can accomplish anything.

Our prayers must do something in us before they do something for us. They must affect us before they influence any person or condition. Prayer is a way of working with God. Prayer gives God a new person to work with, in a new situation. When we reach out we open our lives to the purposes of the Eternal. There is safety in God's purposes. There is peace, power, and pardon when we reside within God's purposes. Our prayers have a way of roping us and dragging us back when we step beyond the safety zone.

Prayer does not change God, but it will get you into an attitude to accept what God is ready to do to meet your needs. Praying is a lot like turning on a radio. The sound waves are already in the air. The room is full of whatever the radio is transmitting but you cannot hear it. When you tune in and reach the right place on the dial the music comes in loud and clear. God's answers are all around us. He does not have to change. But so many times we have to adjust or be adjusted. There is a difference between saying a prayer and praying a prayer. We say a prayer out of duty, but we pray a prayer out of need. When we feel needy, we pray best. When people hurt you, permit your pain to drive you to your knees. The blessings and the answers are already there. God goes before us as a guiding light and lingers behind us with this protecting hand.

Mining for diamonds does not create diamonds. The diamonds are there long before we search, but when we search for them in the right place, we find them. Our search did not create the diamonds, but it brought us to the right place to be rewarded. This is the truth about prayer. Prayer does not create anything. It does not change God; it brings us to a place of great rewards.

God knows us better than to overdo anything. An overload of diamonds would decrease their value. Sometimes we are cast into places by people who do not care for us, yet their deeds force us to search out precious stones of unmeasured blessings.

When we feel the need for help, true prayer takes us to the place where help is. No, our prayers will not change God, but they will produce a change in us. And as we change, we will discover those wonderful blessings that are filling our rooms and saturating the very ground beneath our feet. When people hurt you, you do not have to hate. You can pray! You do not have to loose your cool. You can pray! You do not have to curse, kick, or strike. You can tune into heavenly resources. You can mine heavenly gems because you can pray. You can pray out loud. You can pray silently. You can pray with your eyes open or you can pray with your eyes closed. You can pray sitting down or standing up. Your prayers will fix you, and sometimes they will fix your problems. Sometimes God fixes you without fixing the problem so it will drive you to uncover some gems that would otherwise go unknown. Mining for diamonds is not pleasant work. But when you realize the goal, the toil of the process diminishes. The things that are really worth having can be yours if you are devoted to prayer.

Prayer brings God to us as fresh air rushes into a stagnant room through an open window. The open window did not change the air but it did refresh the room. God is full of power. Prayer appropriates a part of what God is. Prayer can do anything that God can do.

A sailor was confronted with the task of trying to tell a small boy about sailing on the sea. He told the boy about the wind. The boy asked, "What's wind?" The sailor responded, "I don't know what wind is myself, but I do know what it does when I raise my sail." The winds of God's grace are always blowing. When we pray, we are lifting our sails. The winds of God's wisdom and power will propel us to a better place of spiritual insight. We cannot tell the wind to blow east or west. Our task as Christians is to learn how to adjust our sails so that we will travel in the right direction.

A farmer once had a weather vane on the top of his barn. The vane had an arrow that always pointed in the direction from which the wind was blowing. He had a message fastened to the arrow which read "God is love." The farmer was questioned concerning the purpose in attaching such a message to an arrow that was at the mercy of every vagrant wind. When he responded to his questioner, he replied that he attached the message because "God is love no matter what direction the wind blows."

The love of God is unchangeable regardless of how the wind blows. Circumstances change. People move on. Life in this world is made up of highs and lows, bitter and sweet; but the abiding reality of an unchanging love from the source of all blessings can revive and renew. When we truly accept the fact that God's love is ours regardless of our lot, we become changed people.

The parable of the prodigal son found in Luke 15 dramatically illustrates a great truth. When life was good, the young man was only concerned about getting. He went to his father with a selfish request. As I read the story, he was not even polite in his request. In psychology there is a phrase called a "narcissistic entitlement." A narcissistic entitlement is a belief born out of excessive self-admiration and self-love. This person believes that he should be entitled to nothing less than the best.

This phrase is borrowed from Greek mythology. The Greek story of Narcissus was that he was given a beauty so rare that he was not permitted to ever look at himself. One day, he went to the spring for a drink of water. As he drank, he saw a reflection of himself in the water. He was so overwhelmed that he fell in love with himself and he eventually drowned trying to secure the reflection of himself.

Excessive self-admiration not only harms us, it will eventually kill us as it did Narcissus. The prodigal son was broken of his self-absorption by the rough treatment that he received in the "far country." He fell hard. And it was his suffering condition that humbled him. It did not feel good to be at the hog trough, but it worked out for his good. He grew up. He developed spiritually. He matured admirably, and he said, "I will arise, go to my father and say, make me one of thy hired servants." There are a lot of things that are good for you that are not good to you.

Prayer that brings power is prayer that is not trying to change the mind of God. Real prayer is concerned more about discovering God's will than it is about changing God's mind.

The Model Prayer

After this manner therefore pray ye: "Our Father which art in heaven, hollowed be thy name. Thy kingdom come. Thy will be done in earth, as it is in heaven. Give us this day our daily bread. And forgive us our debts, as we forgive our debtors. And lead us not into temptation, but deliver us from evil: for thine is the kingdom, and the power, and the glory, forever. Amen" (Matt. 6:9-13).

This was Jesus' prayer. It was never intended to be our daily prayer. Jesus said, "Pray after this manner," not pray using these words. This prayer is a pattern — not a substitute — for personal prayer. We are not to simply recite these words. We are to use them as a guide in our own personal prayer life. The spirit of this prayer provides power when we catch it and allow ourselves to be ruled by it. It is easy to memorize sacred words, but it is not always easy to pray them. A prayer should lift us out of our personal obsessions.

We are told to pray, "Our Father," and for the rest of the prayer we are directed to say, "Give us," "forgive us," "lead us," and "deliver us." This kind of praying lifts us out of self. You cannot pray like this and nurse a personal wound. This kind of praying makes God's will, God's kingdom, God's name, and God's people so prevalent that the person who prays "after this manner" loses sight of selfish goals. The kingdom of God is bigger than a person. The will of God is greater and far better than anything of human origin. The bread that God measures out is not only daily bread, it is community bread. We each have personal needs, but those personal needs are met only when God's name is hallowed. You see, what God does in us and through us is far more important than what He does for us in our post salvation state.

Peace in Our Babylon

Jeremiah 29:7 says, "And seek the peace of the city whither I have caused you to be carried away captives, and pray unto the Lord for it: for in the peace thereof shall ye have peace." God might not get us out of trouble, but when we pray rightly He will get the trouble out of us. God's people were sent to Babylon for a period of seventy years. It was while they were in that state of captivity that they dropped the habit and sin of idolatry. They were captives cut off from their native soil. They were locked into a disconcerting set up, yet God promised to provide them with peace in the city of their captivity. It is not difficult to picture them at peace on the snow-capped mountains of Jerusalem. It is not a tough assignment to envision them at peace as they strolled amidst the massive cedars of Lebanon. It is not difficult to imagine a peaceful glow emulating from a worshiper sitting in the inner courts of the temple. But God says to his people, "If you pray I can and I will give you peace in Babylon — the city of your captivity." When people do you wrong, when the whole world seems to be against you, God says, "I can give you peace." You do not have to pretend. God is able to give you peace wherever you are. When we are placed in our various places of captivity we must not exclude prayer from our agenda. We must not wear our feelings on our shoulders. Someone has well said, "Some people live like they are on top of the world and others live like the whole world is on top of them." When dreams turn to ashes, when you are pushed back behind your own goal line, "There is," God says, "a peace that can reach you where you are." This is not simply my prophecy but this is God's promise.

- Eleven -

Model Prayers to Be Prayed When Wronged

The purpose of these prayers rest not in providing you with the exact words of prayer, rather to enable you to catch the correct spirit of prayer. Once again, I must emphasize that I am not writing from some expensive seat in the stadium, but from the playing field. I know the pain. I have felt the bruises. I have lived with the numbness, as you have or will in the future. The care of God is both far reaching and finely tuned. Nothing is over unless God says it is over. Neither the prophets of doom nor the victims of fear have the last word. I should also say in the same breath that even you do not have the last word. You cannot always trust your feelings, but you can always trust God.

Prayer When Wronged Romantically

Heavenly Father, I have fears that I now confess to You, that I dare not share with others. My world seems to be coming apart, and I do not know what it means. My heart is breaking, and I pray that it is only breaking to be mended for a greater purpose than I have known. I feel weary, and I pray for rest that is in keeping with Your heavenly will and according to that mysterious measure of my own needs. I ask You to save me from bitterness, yet strengthen my resolve to live beyond this pain. Help me examine both my assets and my limitations. The perfect match seems to have made a perfect mess. And it is a mess I cannot bear with my own strength. It is a mess that I cannot overcome in my own wisdom. I need Thee. I bless Your name and pray for the grace to see Christ beyond this crisis. I have been wronged, but I thank You that You have not deserted me. Lord keep my heart. Please hold my feeble, hand for I do not trust my hand to hold on to You. In the name of our Christ, I claim the victory that is coming and the blessing that never leaves. In the name of our Christ I pray. Amen.

Prayer When Wronged By a Relative

Creator of all the families of the earth, I thank Thee that Jesus Christ never meets a stranger. You know my condition. You see my disappointment. You understand my surprise, and You alone feel my sorrow. Why people change is a mystery to me, but how they walk is no puzzle to You. My soul is sorrowful. The ground that I have walked across safely in past days seems to be giving way beneath my feet. You made the institution of the family, and You alone can make it work right and fix it when it is broken. I feel cut off, yet I know that I can be held up. I pray for Your forgiveness to reside in my heart so I will not be enslaved by the wrong committed against me. I pray for Your patience to overrule my impatience so I might be prepared to see the trophy that will be won. I know that You can bring good out of evil, right out of wrong, and peace out of confusion. Lord, make me strong enough to move when I need to, and teach me how to wait until I am sure of Your call to seize the moment. Father, teach me to say nothing when nothing is best, and guide my spoken words in a way that will heal the hurt and glorify Your name. In the name of our Christ, I pray. Amen.

Prayer When Wronged By a Deceitful Friend

Heavenly Father, I address You as Jehovah-Shalom because You are the only source of lasting peace. I pray in this painful disaster that rebuild my faith in the decency of people and I claim Your aid in my struggle. I pledge my allegiance to Your reign in this world and seek Your guidance in choosing my friends. Heal my anger, and clear my eyes that I might see a gift in this unlikely package. If there are changes that I must make, guide me as I execute them. If there are fences that I must mend, work in me that my labor will not be in vain. If there are reports that I must confront, speak through me that my spirit will not sabotage my goal. If there is gossip that I must live through, make me wise enough to overcome and strong enough to outlive. I pray for a sensitive and caring spirit that I can hear the cries of others who hurt in ways deeper than I have known. I pray for Your divine presence, for I know that everything is so right with You that it will affect whatever is wrong with me. I pray for my deceitful friend that Your light might outshine the darkness of this deceitful deed. In the name of Him who is our peace, I pray. Amen.

Prayer When Wronged By Someone You Have Helped

Almighty God, I praise Your name because You have spoken well of the days to come. The days of my past have known a heaviness of heart that has come from an unexpected place. My kindness has been repaid with kindness. My help has been rewarded by hurt. I ask you to dry the tears that no hand but Yours can touch. I know that Your image is upon me, and You will not forsake that which You have redeemed. You have marked my life by a glorious sign that I cannot mistake. I know that no person is ineligible for forgiveness or forbidden to receive kindness. I have given sincerely, and I ask that you would bless my purpose and overrule my repayment. Heavenly Father, You know where I am strong and where I am weak. You know the door which is closed to Satan and the window through which he comes with unmeasured knowledge. I ask You for the strength to put on the whole armor of God. Please give me a new vision of glory and let not this pain separate me from those who truly need my help and will be thankful for the same. I know that Your law is love and I thank You that even when I question Your grace You always find ways to overcome my suspicions. In the name of our Christ, I pray. Amen.

Prayer When Wronged By an Open Enemy

Heavenly Father, in Thy Word Thou hast said, "Woe unto you when all men speak well of you." Living in a world as we live, I take comfort in believing that I must be doing something right. I feel the force of open hatred, yet I find no fear. I believe that You are with me, and because of Your presence, even the valley becomes high ground. I know that my fight is not with flesh and blood but with spiritual wickedness in high places. I need a guide who has walked this path without stumbling. I need a tried friend upon whom I can lean, with whom I can live through this untried test and unknown battle. The only victory I seek is the one that You will give. The only peace I will accept is that which abides in You. The only weapons I will use are those that come from You. The only rest I trust is that which men cannot disturb. Help me to make the right choices and keep the vows that I made to You and to myself. I have been reached by a cruel deed, but I pray that I will not be ruled by it. Help me remember that vengeance belongs to You because You alone avenge with perfect justice. Let Your life and Your light abide in me. In the name of our Christ, I pray. Amen.

Prayer When Wronged By Lying Lips

God of all truth, I thank Thee that You know the truth about me. Help me take comfort in the knowledge You possess and the future Your knowledge will make for me. I know that nothing can withstand Your power. In my heart I believe that no cross is too heavy, no mountain is too steep, and no problems are too many.

I look to You, the Master of all circumstances, to clear up that which is not clear and to straighten out that which is crooked. No plot pieced and woven together by evil influences can be successful when You decree their ends.

Heavenly Father, I know that Your will is more important than my feelings. I understand that I am only traveling a way that You have already examined. When people called you by heart-breaking names and treated You with mind baffling contempt You rose beyond their mockery. I pray at this hour for the strength, power, and peace to do the same. Let these false reports become gates through which I pass rather than fences within which I sulk. I know that Your plan is greater than my pain. I pray for the wisdom to walk in a way that will glorify Your name and will refute that which is spoken by evil lips. I claim the sufficiency of Your grace and the sweetness of Your presence and will fear no evil because Thou art with me. In the name of our Christ, I pray. Amen.

Prayer When Wronged By Jealous Acquaintances

Father of all lights, I know that You are the giver of every good and perfect gift. I thank Thee for those gifts showered upon me by Your loving hands. I feel that cost of having received those blessings by the attacks from envious and jealous people around me. You are always right, and if given a choice, I will prefer to be blessed by You and resented by the jealous. Dear God, You have taught us in Your Word that it is by great tribulation that we enter the kingdom. You have been good to me. I have been blessed beyond my expectations. I know that I have not been lucky, but I have been led and favored by You. I thank You that man did not make me. I thank You that people cannot stop me. I praise You that Satan cannot destroy me. I am Yours and all that You have turned my way is Yours.

I pray for the jealous. Help them to see their own blessings. Help them to come to a foundation that never shakes and a fountain that never runs dry. I know that Your blessings do not leave You with less and what you have done in my life can be done in greater ways in the lives of others. Help me to be kind when greeted with unkind acts. Help me to be humble as I interact with the haughty, and please use me as I seek to be a living witness of the fact that You can do anything but fail. In the name of our Christ, I pray. Amen.

Prayer When Wronged By the Silence of Someone Who Should Speak Up for You

O God of infinite love, I thank You that there is no failure in You. A voice is silent that could speak on my behalf. A helping hand is far from helping that is not far at all. I know that the human solution is not the only remedy. My life is divinely ordered, and I am not afraid. My strength is always present in Your supreme completeness. I acknowledge Your presence and Your power even as I feel this human neglect. I do not see the good in it but I know that You can bring good out of it. Teach me how to go on without being resentful. Guide me, that my steps will be spiritual and my words will be measured.

I thank Thee that I am not left into the hands of flesh and blood but through Your providence I know that I can be picked up, brushed off, and reestablished on higher planes that I can imagine. I praise You that the last word about this crisis is with You. I know that people can be weak. I have felt my weakness and the outcomes of the same. I am reminded once again that anything and anybody less than God will let me down. My soul is Your classroom and my discomfort is nothing more than Your opportunity. Bless my friends! Bless my family and please, bless my enemies with a knowledge of You. I know that one day we shall know the truth and the truth will set us free. In the name of Him who never fails, I ask it all. Amen.

Prayer to Forgive Someone Whom You Thought You Had, But You Have Not

God of all mercies, I have tried to forgive, but in my heart I have not let go. I do not know if I can. The hurt seems so big and I feel so small that I must ask You to forgive through me. Father, make me a channel of Your forgiveness. I do not want to live in the past, yet I am not free to benefit from the beauty and blessings of present. I know in my head what I ought to do, yet I feel in my heart the pains for what I have not done. I am weak, but You are strong. Heal my insufficiency, and do in me that which I cannot do in my own strength. I want nothing to stand between You and me. I want no walls to separate us and no sins to distance us. I want You more than I want to have my way. I need You more than I need to keep this pain. Help me to let go and receive more of Your spirit. Teach me how to make room for love and to dispel resentment. You could have hurled me away like a shepherd without a tent, but instead You have renewed my opportunities to move on. I thank Thee for Thy patience and I will not permit it to be wasted. I forgive _____ (person's name), not in my name because I am here for only a while, but in the precious sin forgiving name of Jesus Christ, my Savior and my Lord. Amen.

Prayer When Wronged on a Job

Eternal God, I thank You that You are God everywhere. There is no place that excludes You, and there is no office that is above You. Familiar people seem unfamiliar, and my job feels like a journey into a far country. I am confronted with my helplessness. I feel the threat. I sense an effort to cut me off and cut me out, and I do not know what it all means. I see some of what is happening, but I cannot see where it will ultimately go or where it will eventually stop. Yet, in the midst of this uncertainty, I am reminded that I have a sure anchor and a solid future because of You. I thank You that I am not in the hands of a grim and speechless fate; rather in the hands of a loving heavenly Father. I know that all kinds of things happen to all kinds of people but Your word says all things work together for good to them that love the Lord.

At this hour, at this time, in this crisis, I rededicate myself to loving You more than I love anything that this world can offer or take away. For in Your Word You did not say some things or a few things, but You said all things would work together for good to them that love You. Whatever happens on this job must be related to the grand strategy which You are working out in my life. I praise You for the outcome that I cannot create and people cannot hinder. Tomorrow is another day, and I greet it by saying not my will but Thine be done; in earth, even as it is in heaven. I know You will provide my daily bread even as You have given me my daily strength. In the name of our Christ, I pray. Amen.

Prayer When Wronged By a Religious Figure

Holy and Heavenly God, whose Grace has no limit and whose power has no boundary, I know that the real test of my faith is not how I feel after church, but how I act in the world in which I live. At this moment, I feel as though I have been wounded by the claws of a deceitful wolf dressed in the most attractive sheep's clothing. This was one I trusted and respected. My trust has been betrayed. My respect has been shattered. My confidence has been shaken.

Empower me now, Father, so I will not settle for my state of brokenness. In the name of Jesus, who was above us and became God walking beside us and living where we are now living, I gather up the fragments from this sad encounter. I lay my head on Your wisdom and my hunger in Your abundance. The mountain that I must climb, is steep enough without the weight of resentment in my heart. I know that this person who hurt me did not do so at Your bidding. Whether this deed comes from a false prophet or a weak leader, only You can judge. You know the whole story, I do not. You see the whole picture, I cannot. But just as Nehemiah built the walls of Jerusalem, in troublesome times, I pray for the grace to do my work in my time and let You settle the score. I am Your witness, not Your prosecutor.

I know, Father, that Your Love is an action toward us and not a reaction to us. You do not change us so You can love us, but You love us so that You can change us. And as I pray these words I am reminded of the fact that You can use imperfect people in spite of themselves. I will, in spite of my disappointment, act according to Your directive and not react according to my pain. "Speak Lord. For thy servant hearest." In the living name of our living Lord, I pray. Amen.

Prayer When Wronged By a Misunderstanding

I give You thanks, O God, that You decreed that our Lord would walk life's road before us. I pause to remember that our Lord knew hard work and misunderstandings. As I seek to follow You in obedience, this confusion and trouble has been manifested in my life. I come before You confessing that I have exhausted all of my resources for changing this misunderstanding and have found out that I am powerless to change this disconcerting set up.

As Jesus drew apart from the crowds to think and pray, seeking Your direction, I come at this hour seeking guidance and strength for this challenge that I cannot overcome. Father of all grace, I know that at Your holy word storms are stilled, diseases are healed, and even the dead are raised. Grant, I pray, Almighty God, that by Your mercy such faith will so rest within my heart that possibilities will become facts.

As I seek to out live this wrong that has been done, enable me to live out my faith and cheer those who are suffering in greater ways than I am, by my sympathy for them. I know that Your will is best. Through this misunderstanding, I ask for greater strength to offer some kindness to others without any feeling of self-righteousness, for no cause except that of

Christian love. From You alone I can learn the true meaning of life and the place of this misunderstanding in my life. I thank You, Father, that we cannot escape Your judgment and neither can we flee from Your far reaching love. Through Your kingdom on this earth, Your light shines in every corner. I will seek your face and trust the outcome to Your hands. In the blessed name of Him who is our Peace, Amen.

Prayer When Hurt By Someone Who Is Weak, But Not Wicked

O, invisible and immortal God, You have created us to seek You, and You alone have put deep within us the hope of finding You. In Your Word You said of Your sleepy-eyed disciples, "The spirit is willing, but the flesh is weak." You see the good that others miss. You know our hearts and our hearts desires. Great and living God, please hear my prayers. I recognize Your majesty. I delight to sing Your praise. My petition is simple. Please overrule the weakness of the flesh, and reign in that life that is in desperate need of your strength.

Heavenly Father, I believe that Christ took the place of every thief who ever denied You of what is rightfully Yours. Jesus Christ, Your only begotten son, has paid in full for every act of spiritual larceny ever committed. In Your Son, Jesus Christ, You chose to buy back what was rightfully Yours. You have, by Your grace and mercy, canceled the note of all pilfering indebtedness. Lord, You have fixed it where the strength of heaven's vaulted powers have swung open at the confession of those who would give to You that which belongs to You. You have taught us to pray for the weak. I obey Your Word. I trust Your wisdom. I am reminded that we can be gathered together in victory over all that can defeat us by Him whose holy arms encircle us all. In Jesus name, I pray. Amen.

Prayer When Wronged By a Spouse

Heavenly Father, whose Word is infallible and whose power is unlimited, I am caught between giving up and going on. My misery, at this moment, seems to do more to me than I can evaluate. My mate, who is a part of me, has hurt that which is the rest of me. As I seek to sift and to sort, I more intensely feel my need for Your guidance. I know that marriage is holy in Your sight, and, at this moment, I seek to "abide under the shadow of the Almighty." I do so, Father, because I need a place to hide and a place to heal. My marriage, at this time, is like a party that has run out of joy. I am going through motions that have no glad meaning. I want that happiness that seems to be so elusive. I want that dream of young love to be realized. I want those safe hands that I once thought existed to hold my heart.

I have stepped into the place of the unknown. I have no predictions and I do not know how to make plans for a future that I cannot envision. Father, You said that, "the Valley of Achor could become a door of hope." You promised to transform a place where the stones of judgment had fallen into a place where benedictions of grace would descend. I trust Your tender kindness to turn my tears into rejoicing and despair into hope. I see your promise as a cameo revealing the enlarging grace of Your unlimited strength.

Whatever I must do, lead me in that direction. For, Lord, if You lead, I know that I will be led right. I pray for my spouse and I lay this marriage, "for better or for worse," at your feet. Not my will, but Thine be done, in my home and in my heart, even as it is done in heaven. In the name of our blessed Savior Jesus Christ, I pray. Amen.

PROMISES
YOU CAN COUNT ON . . .

When You Are Feeling Alone

Deuteronomy 5:29-31

O that there were such an heart in them, that they would fear me, and keep all my commandments always, that it might be well with them, and with their children for ever!

Go say to them, Get you into your tents again.

But as for thee, stand thou here by me, and I will speak unto thee all the commandments, and the statutes, and the judgments, which thou shalt teach them, that they may do them in the land which I give them to possess it.

Deuteronomy 31:6

Be strong of a good courage, fear not, nor be afraid of them: for the Lord thy God, he it is that doth go with thee; he will not fail thee, nor forsake thee.

1 Samuel 12:22

For the Lord will not forsake his people for his great name's sake: because it hath pleased the Lord to make you his people.

Psalm 23:1

The Lord is my shepherd; I shall not want.

Isaiah 54:10-14

For the mountains shall depart, and the hills be removed; but my kindness shall not depart from thee, neither shall the covenant of my peace be removed, saith the Lord that hath mercy on thee,

O thou afflicted, tossed with tempest, and not comforted, behold, I will lay thy stones with fair colours, and lay they foundations with sapphires.

And I will make thy windows of agates, and thy gates of carbuncles, and all thy borders of pleasant stones.

And all thy children shall be taught of the Lord; and great shall be the peace of thy children.

In righteousness shalt thou be established: thou shalt be far from oppression; for thou shalt not fear: and from terror; for it shall not come near thee.

John 14:16-18

And I will pray the Father, and he shall give you another Comforter, that he may abide with you for ever;

Even the Spirit of the truth; whom the world cannot receive because it seeth him not, neither knoweth him: but ye know him; for he dwelleth with you, and shall be in you.

I will not leave you comfortless: I will come to you.

Hebrews 13:5

Let your conversation be without covetousness; and be content with such things as ye have: for he hath said, I will never leave thee, nor forsake thee.

1 Peter 5:6-11

Humble yourselves therefore under the mighty hand of God, that he may exalt you in due time:

Casting all your care upon him; for he careth for you.

Be sober, be vigilant; because your adversary the devil, as a roaring lion, walketh about, seeking whom he may devour:

Whom resist steadfast in the faith, knowing that the same afflictions are accomplished in your brethren that are in the world.

But the God of all grace, whom hath called us unto his eternal glory by Christ Jesus, after that ye have suffered a while, make you perfect, stablish, strengthen, settle you.

To him be glory and domination for ever and ever. Amen.

When You Are Feeling Angry

Psalm 37:8

Cease from anger, and forsake wrath: fret not thyself in any wise to do evil.

Proverbs 14:16-17

A wise man feareth, and departeth from evil: but the fool rageth, and is confident.

He that is soon angry dealeth foolishly: and a man of wicked devices is hated.

Proverbs 15:1, 18

A soft answer turneth away wrath: but grievous words stir up anger.

A wrathful man stirreth up strife: but he that is slow to anger appeaseth strife.

Proverbs 16:32

He that is slow to anger is better than the mighty; and he that ruleth his spirit than he that taketh a city.

Proverbs 22:24-25

Make no friendship with an angry man; and with a furious man thou shalt not go:

Lest thou learn his ways, and get a snare to thy soul.

Proverbs 25: 21-22

If thine enemy be hungry, give him bread to eat; and if he be thirsty, give him water to drink:

For thou shalt heap coals of fire upon his head, and the Lord shall reward thee.

Proverbs 29:22

An angry man stirreth up strife, and a furious man aboundeth in transgression.

Ecclesiastes 7:9

Be not hasty in thy spirit to be angry: for anger resteth in the bosom of fools.

Matthew 5:22

But I say unto you, That whosoever is angry with his brother without cause shall be in danger of the judgment: and whosoever shall be in danger of the council: but whosoever shall say to his brother, Raca, shall be in danger of the council: but whosoever shall say, thou fool, shall be in danger of hell fire.

Romans 12:17-21

Recompense to no man evil for evil. Provide things honest in the sight of all men.

If it be possible, as much as lieth in you, live peaceably with all men.

Dearly beloved, avenge not yourselves, but rather give place unto wrath: for it is written, Vengeance is mine; I will repay, saith the Lord.

Therefore if thine enemy hunger, feed him; if he thirst, give him drink: for in so doing thou shalt heap coals of fire on his head.

Be not overcome of evil, but overcome evil with good.

Ephesians 4:26, 31-32

Let all bitterness, and wrath, and anger, and clamour, and evil speaking, be put away from you, with all malice:

And be ye kind, one to another, tenderhearted, forgiving one another, even as God for Christ's sake hath forgiven you.

Colossians 3:8

But now ye also put off all these; anger, wrath, malice, blasphemy, filthy communication out of your mouth.

James 1:19, 20

Wherefore, my beloved brethren, let every man be swift to hear, slow to speak, slow to wrath:

For the wrath of man worketh not the righteousness of God.

When You Are in Need of Comfort

Genesis 28:15

And, behold, I am with thee, and will keep thee in all places whither thou goest, and will bring thee again into this land; for I will not leave thee, until I have done that which I have spoken to thee of.

Numbers 23:19

God is not a man, that he should lie; neither the son of man, that he should repent: hath he said, and shall he not do it? or hath he spoken, and shall he not make it good?

1 Kings 8:56

Blessed be the Lord, that hath given rest unto his people Israel, according to all that he promised: there hath not failed one word of all his good promise, which he promised by the hand of Moses his servant.

Nehemiah 8:10

Then he said unto them, Go your way, eat the fat, and drink the sweet, and send portions unto them for whom nothing is prepared: for this day is holy unto our Lord: neither be ye sorry; for the joy of the Lord is your strength.

Psalm 30:5

For his anger endureth but a moment; in his favour is life: weeping may endure for a night, but joy cometh in the morning.

Psalm 46:1-3

God is our refuge and strength, a very present help in trouble.

Therefore will not we fear, though the earth be removed, and though the mountains be carried into the midst of the sea;

Isaiah 41:10

Fear thou not; for I am with thee: be not dismayed; for I am thy God: I will strengthen thee; yea, I will help thee; yea, I will uphold thee with the right hand of my righteousness.

Matthew 11:28-30

Come unto me, all ye that labour and are heavy laden, and I will give you rest.

Take my yoke upon you, and learn of me; for I am meek and lowly in heart: and ye shall find rest unto your souls.

For my yoke is easy, and my burden is light.

2 Corinthians 1:3-4

Blessed be God, even the Father of our Lord Jesus Christ, the Father of mercies, and the God of all comfort;

Who comforteth us in all our tribulation, that we may be able to comfort them which are in any trouble, by the comfort wherewith we ourselves are comforted of God.

1 Peter 4:12-13

Beloved, think it not strange concerning the fiery trial which is to try you, as though some strange thing happened unto you:

But rejoice, inasmuch as ye are partakers of Christ's sufferings; that, when his glory shall be revealed, ye may be glad also with exceeding joy.

2 Peter 3:9

The Lord is not slack concerning his promise, as some men count slackness; but is longsuffering to us-ward, not willing that any should perish, but that all should come to repentance.

When You Need Reassurance
That Evil Will Not Prevail

2 King 6:15-17

And when the servant of the man of God was risen early, and gone forth, behold, an host compassed the city both with horses and chariots. And his servant said unto him, Alas, my master! how shall we do?

And he answered, Fear not: for they that be with us are more than they that be with them.

And Elisha prayed, and said, Lord, I pray thee, open his eyes, that he may see. And the Lord opened the eyes of the young man; and he saw: and behold, the mountain was full of horses and chariots of fire round about Elisha.

Psalm 7:11-12

God judgeth the righteous, and God is angry with the wicked every day.

If he turn not, he will whet his sword; he hath bent his bow, and made it ready.

Psalm 23:4-5

Yea, though I walk through the valley of the shadow of death, I will fear no evil: for thou art with me; thy rod and thy staff they comfort me.

Thou preparest a table before me in the presence of mine enemies: thou anointest my head with oil; my cup runneth over.

Psalm 27:1-2

The Lord is my light and my salvation; whom shall I fear? the Lord is the strength of my life; of whom shall I be afraid?

When the wicked, even mine enemies and my foes, came upon me to eat up my flesh, they stumbled and fell.

Psalm 91:1-7

He that dwelleth in the secret place of the most High shall abide under the shadow of the Almighty.

I will say of the Lord, He is my refuge and my fortress: my God, in him will I trust.

Surely he shall deliver thee from the snare of the fowler, and from the noisome pestilence.

He shall cover thee with his feathers, and under his wings shalt thou trust: his truth shall be thy shield and buckler.

Thou shalt not be afraid for the terror by night; nor for the arrow that flieth by day;

Nor for the pestilence that walketh in darkness; nor for the destruction that wasteth at noonday.

A thousand shall fall at thy side, and ten thousand at thy right hand; but it shall not come nigh thee.

Isaiah 41:10-16

Fear thou not; for I am with thee: be not dismayed; for I am thy God: I will strengthen thee; yea, I will help thee; yea, I will uphold thee with the right hand of my righteousness.

Behold, all they that were incensed against thee shall be ashamed and confounded: they shall be as nothing; and they that strive with thee shall perish.

Thou shalt seek them, and shalt not find them, even them that contended with thee: they that war against thee shall be as nothing, and as a thing of naught.

For I the Lord thy God will hold thy right hand, saying unto thee, Fear not; I will help thee.

Fear not, thou worm Jacob, and ye men of Israel; I will help thee, saith the Lord, and thy Redeemer, the Holy One of Israel.

Behold, I will make thee a new sharp threshing instrument having teeth: thou shalt thresh the mountains, and beat them small, and shalt make the hills as chaff.

Thou shalt fan them, and the wind shall carry them away, and the whirlwind shall scatter them: and thou shalt rejoice in the Lord, and shalt glory in the Holy One of Israel.

Isaiah 43:1-2

But now thus saith the Lord that created thee, O Jacob, and he that formed thee, O Israel, Fear not: for I have redeemed thee, I have called thee by thy name; thou art mine.

When Thou passest through the waters, I will be with thee; and through the rivers, they shall not overflow thee: when thou walkest through fire, thou shalt not be burned; neither shall the flame kindle upon thee.

Isaiah 50:8-10

He is near that justifieth me; who will contend with me? let us stand together: who is mine adversary? let him come near to me.

Behold, the Lord God will help me; who is he that shall condemn me? lo, they all shall wax old as a garment; the moth shall eat them up.

Who is among you that feareth the Lord, that obeyeth the voice of his servant, that walketh in darkness, and hath no light? let him trust in the name of the Lord, and stay upon his God.

Isaiah 51:11-12

Therefore the redeemed of the Lord shall return, and come with singing unto Zion; and everlasting joy shall be upon their head: they shall obtain gladness and joy; and sorrow and mourning shall flee away.

I, even I, am he that comforteth you: who are thou, that thou shouldest be afraid of a man that shall die, and of the son of man which shall be made as grass;

Romans 8:31, 35-39

What shall we then say to these things? If God be for us, who can be against us?

Who shall separate us from the love of Christ? shall tribulation, or distress, or persecution, or famine, or nakedness, or peril, or sword?

As it is written, For thy sake we are killed all the day long; we are accounted as sheep for the slaughter.

Nay, in all these things we are more than conquerors through him that loved us.

For I am persuaded, that neither death, nor life, nor angels, nor principalities, nor powers, nor things present, nor things to come,

Nor height, nor depth, not any other creature, shall be able to separate us from the love of God, which is in Christ Jesus our Lord.

1 Peter 3:12-14

For the eyes of the Lord are over the righteous, and his ears are open unto their prayers: but the face of the Lord is against them that do evil.

And who is he that will harm you, if ye be followers of that which is good?

But and if ye suffer for righteousness' sake, happy are ye: and be not afraid of their terror, neither be troubled;

Romans 8:31, 35-39

What shall we then say to these things? If God be for us, who can be against us?

Who shall separate us from the love of Christ? shall tribulation, or distress, or persecution, or famine, or nakedness, or peril, or sword?

As it is written, For thy sake we are killed all the day long; we are accounted as sheep for the slaughter.

Nay, in all these things we are more than conquerors through him that loved us.

For I am persuaded, that neither death, nor life, nor angels, nor principalities, nor powers, nor things present, nor things to come,

Nor height, nor depth, not any other creature, shall be able to separate us from the love of God, which is in Christ Jesus our Lord.

Nor for the pestilence that walketh in darkness; nor for the destruction that wasteth at noonday.

1 Peter 3:12-14

For the eyes of the Lord are over the righteous, and his ears are open unto their prayers: but the face of the Lord is against them that do evil.

And who is he that will harm you, if ye be followers of that which is good?

But and if ye suffer for righteousness' sake, happy are ye: and be not afraid of their terror, neither be troubled;

When You Are Feeling Deserted

Deuteronomy 4:31

(For the Lord thy God is a merciful God;) he will not forsake thee, neither destroy thee, nor forget the covenant of thy fathers which he sware unto them.

Psalm 17:8-9

Keep me as the apple of the eye, hide me under the shadow of thy wings,

From the wicked that oppress me, from my deadly enemies, who compass me about.

Psalm 18:28-29

For thou wilt light my candle: the Lord my God will enlighten my darkness.

For by thee I have run through a troop; and by my God have I leaped over a wall.

Psalm 30:4-5

Sing unto the Lord, O ye saints of his, and give thanks at the remembrance of his holiness.

For his anger endureth but a moment; in his favour is life: weeping may endure for a night, but joy cometh in the morning.

Psalm 32:7

Thou art my hiding place; thou shalt preserve me from trouble; thou shalt compass me about with songs of deliverance. Selah.

Psalm 34:18-19

The Lord is nigh unto them that are of a broken heart; and saveth such as be of a contrite spirit.

Many are the afflictions of the righteous: but the Lord delivereth him out of them all.

Psalm 91:14-15

Because he hath set his love upon me, therefore will I deliver him: I will set him on high, because he hath known my name.

He shall call upon me, and I will answer him: I will be with him in trouble, I will deliver him, and honour him.

Psalm 126:5-6

They that sow in tears shall reap in joy.

He that goeth forth and weepeth, bearing precious seed, shall doubtless come again with rejoicing, bringing his sheaves with him.

Isaiah 43:2

When thou passest through the waters, I will be with thee; and through the rivers, they shall not overflow thee: when thou walkest through the fire, thou shalt not be burned; neither shall the flame kindle upon thee.

Isaiah 49:15-16

Can a woman forget her sucking child, that she should not have compassion on the son of her womb? yea, they may forget, yet will I not forget thee.

Behold, I have graven thee upon the palms of my hands; thy walls are continually before me.

Isaiah 62:4

Thou shalt no more be termed Forsaken; neither shall thy land any more be termed Desolate: but thou shalt be called Hephzibah and thy land Beulah: for the Lord delighteth in thee, and thy land shall be married.

When You Need to Know Good Can Come Out of Evil

Genesis 31:41-42

Thus I have been twenty years in thy house; I served thee fourteen years for thy two daughters, and six years for thy cattle: and thou hast changed my wages ten times.

Except the God of my father, the God of Abraham, and the fear of Isaac, had been with me, surely thou hadst sent me away now empty. God hasth seen mine affliction and the labour of my hands, and rebuked thee yesternight.

Genesis 50:18-20

And his brethren also went and fell down before his face; and they said, Behold, we be thy servants.

And Joseph said unto them, Fear not: for am I in the place of God?

But as for you, ye thought evil against me; but God meant it unto good, to bring to pass it is this day, to save much people alive.

Psalm 119:71

It is good for me that I have been afflicted; that I might learn thy statutes.

Psalm 126:5-6

They that sow in tears shall reap in joy.

He that goeth forth and weepeth; bearing precious seed, shall doubtless come again with rejoicing, bringing his sheaves with him.

Habakkuk 3:17-19

Although the fig tree shall not blossom, neither shall fruit be in the vines; the labour of the olive shall fail, and the fields shall yield no meat; the flock shall be cut off from the fold, and there shall be no herd in the stalls:

Yet I will rejoice in the Lord, I will joy in the God of my salvation.

The Lord God is my strength, and he will make my feet like hinds' feet, and he will make me to walk upon mine high places. To the chief singer of my stringed instruments.

Romans 8:28

And we know that all things work together for good to them that love God, to them who are the called according to his purpose.

Philippians 1:6-12

Being confident of this very thing, that he which hath begun a good work in you will perform it until the day of Jesus Christ:

Even as it is meet for me to think this of you all, because I have you in my heart; inasmuch as both my bonds, and in the defence and confirmation of the gospel, ye all are partakers of my grace.

For God is my record, how greatly I long after you all in the bowels of Jesus Christ.

And this I pray, that your love may abound yet more and more in knowledge and in all judgment;

That ye may approve things are excellent; that ye may be sincere and without offense till the day of Christ;

Being filled with the fruits of righteousness, which are by Jesus Christ, unto the glory and praise of God.

But I would ye should understand, brethren, that the things which happened unto me have fallen out rather unto the furtherance of the gospel;

Revelation 7:13-14

And one of the elders answered, saying unto me, What are these which are arrayed in white robes? And whence came they?

And I said unto him, Sir, thou knowest. And he said to me, These are they which came out of great tribulation, and have washed their robes, and made them white in the blood of the Lamb.

When You Are Feeling Grief

Psalm 23:4

Yea, though I walk through the valley of the shadow of death, I will fear no evil: for thou art with me; thy rod and thy staff they comfort me.

Isaiah 51:11

Therefore the redeemed of the Lord shall return, and come with singing unto Zion; and everlasting joy shall be upon their head: they shall obtain gladness and joy; and sorrow and mourning shall flee away.

Isaiah 61:1-3

The spirit of the Lord God is upon me; because the Lord hath anointed me to preach good tidings unto the meek; he hath sent me to bind up the broken-hearted, to proclaim liberty to the captives, and the opening of the prison to them that are bound;

To proclaim the acceptable year of the Lord, and the day of vengeance of our God; to comfort all that mourn;

To appoint unto them that mourn in Zion, to give unto them beauty for ashes, the oil of joy for mourning, the garment of praise for the spirit of heaviness; that they might be called trees of righteousness, the planting of the Lord, that he might be glorified.

John 14:1-3

Let not your heart be troubled: ye believe in God, believe also in me.

In my Father's house are many mansions: if it were not so, I would have told you. I go to prepare a place for you.

And if I go and prepare a place for you, I will come again, and receive you unto myself; that where I am, there ye may be also.

1 Corinthians 15:55-57

O death, where is thy sting? O grave, where is thy victory? The sting of death is sin; and the strength of sin is the law.

But thanks be to God, which giveth us the victory through our Lord Jesus Christ.

2 Corinthians 1:3-4

Blessed be God, even the Father of our Lord Jesus Christ, the Father of mercies, and the God of all comfort;

Who comforteth us in all our tribulation, that we may be able to comfort them which are in any trouble, by the comfort wherewith we ourselves are comforted of God.

1 Thessalonians 4:13-14

But I would not have you to be ignorant, brethren, concerning them which are asleep, that ye sorrow not, even as others which have not hope.

For if we believe that Jesus died and rose again, even so them also which sleep in Jesus will God bring with him.

Hebrews 4:15-16

For we have not an high priest which cannot be touched with the feelings of our infirmities; but was in all points tempted like as we are, yet without sin.

Let us therefore come boldly unto the throne of grace, that we may obtain mercy, and find grace to help in time of need.

Revelation 21:4

And God shall wipe away all tears from their eyes; and there shall be no more death, neither sorrow, nor crying, neither shall there be any more pain: for the former things are passed away.

When You Are in Need of Guidance

Joshua 1:7-9

Only be thou strong and very courageous, that thou mayest observe to do according to all the law, which Moses my servant commanded thee: turn not from it to the right hand or to the left, that thou mayest prosper whithersoever thou goest.

This book of the law shall not depart out of thy mouth; but thou shalt meditate therein day and night, that thou mayest observe to do according to all that is written therein: for then thou shalt make thy way prosperous, and then thou shalt have good success.

Have not I commanded thee? Be strong and of a good courage; be not afraid, neither be thou dismayed: for the Lord thy God is with thee whithersoever thou goest.

Psalm 32:8-11

I will instruct thee and teach thee in the way which thou shalt go: I will guide thee with mine eye.

Be ye not as the horse, or as the mule, which have no understanding: whose mouth must be held in with bit and bridle, lest they come near unto thee.

Many sorrows shall be to the wicked: but he that trusteth in the Lord, mercy shall compass him about.

Be glad in the Lord, and rejoice, ye righteous: and shout for joy, all ye that are upright in heart.

Psalm 37:23-24

The steps of a good man are ordered by the Lord: and he delighteth in his way.

Though he fall, he shall not be utterly cast down: for the Lord upholdeth him with his hand.

Proverbs 3:3-6

Let not mercy and truth forsake thee: bind them about thy neck; write them upon the table of thine heart:

So shalt thou find favour and good understanding in the sight of God and man.

Trust in the Lord with all thine heart; and lean not unto thine own understanding.

In all thy ways acknowledge him, and he shall direct thy paths.

Proverbs 6:22-23

When thou goest, it shall lead thee; when thou sleepest, it shall keep thee; and when thou awakest, it shall talk with thee.

For the commandment is a lamp; and the law is light; and reproofs of instruction are the way of life:

Isaiah 30:18-21

And therefore will the Lord wait, that he may be gracious unto you, and therefore will he be exalted, that he may have mercy upon you: for the Lord is a God of judgment: blessed are all they that wait for him.

For the people shall dwell in Zion at Jerusalem: thou shalt weep no more: he will be very gracious unto thee at the voice of thy cry; when he shall hear it, he will answer thee.

And though the Lord give you the bread of adversity, and the water of affliction, yet shall not thy teachers be removed into a corner any more, but thine eyes shall see thy teachers.

And thine ears shall hear a word behind thee, saying, This is the way, walk ye in it, when ye turn to the right hand, and when ye turn to the left.

Isaiah 43:16

Thus said the Lord, which maketh a way in the sea, and a path in the mighty waters;

John 8:30-32

As he spake these words, many believed on him.

Then said Jesus to those Jews which believed on him, If ye continue in my word, then are ye my disciples indeed;

And ye shall know the truth, and the truth shall make you free.

When You Are in Need of Patience

Psalm 27:13-14

I had fainted, unless I had believed to see the goodness of the Lord in the land of the living.

Wait on the Lord: be of good courage, and he shall strengthen thine heart: wait, I say, on the Lord.

Psalm 37:8-9

Cease from anger, and forsake wrath: fret not thyself in any wise to do evil.

For evil doers shall be cut off: but those that wait upon the Lord, they shall inherit the earth.

Psalm 46:10-11

Be still, and know that I am God: I will be exalted among the heathen, I will be exalted in the earth.

The Lord of hosts is with us; the God of Jacob is our refuge. Selah.

Ecclesiastes 7:8-9

Better is the end of a thing than the beginning thereof: and the patient in spirit is better than the proud in spirit.

Be not hasty in thy spirit to be angry: for anger resteth in the bosom of fools.

Isaiah 40:28-31

Hast thou not known? hast thou not heard, that the everlasting God, the Lord, the Creator of the ends of the earth, fainteth not, neither is weary? there is no searching of his understanding.

He giveth power to the faint; and to them that have not might he increaseth strength.

Even the youths shall faint and be weary, and the young men shall utterly fall:

But they that wait upon the Lord shall renew their strength; they shall mount up with wings as eagles; they shall run, and not be weary; and they shall walk, and not faint.

Habakkuk 2:1-3

I will stand upon my watch, and set me upon the tower, and will watch to see what he will say unto me, and what I shall answer when I am reproved.

And the Lord answered me, and said, Write the vision, and make it plain upon tables, that he may run that readeth it.

For the vision is yet for an appointed time, but at the end it shall speak, and not though it tarry, wait for it; because it will surely come, it will not tarry.

Romans 5:3-5

And not only so, but we glory in tribulations also: knowing that tribulation worketh patience;

And patience, experience; and experience, hope:

And hope maketh not ashamed; because the love of God is shed abroad in our hearts by the Holy Ghost which is given unto us.

Hebrews 10:8-9

Above when he said, Sacrifice and offering and burn offerings and offering for wouldest not, neither hadst pleasure therein; which are offered by the law;

Then said he, Lo, I come to do thy will, O God. He taketh away the first, that he may establish the second.

Hebrews 12:1

Wherefore seeing we also are compassed about with so great a cloud of witnesses, let us lay aside every weight, and the sin which doth so easily beset us, and let us run with patience the race that is set before us,

James 5:7-8

Be patient therefore, brethren, unto the coming of the Lord. Behold, the husbandman waiteth for the precious fruit of the earth, and hath long patience for it until he receive the early and latter rain.

Be ye also patient; stablish your hearts: for the coming of the Lord draweth nigh.

When You Need Peace of Mind

Psalm 1:1-3

Blessed is the man that walketh not in the counsel of the ungodly, nor standeth in the way of sinners, not sitteth in the seat of the scornful.

But his delight is in the law of the Lord; and in his law doth he meditate day and night.

And he shall be like a tree planted by the rivers of water, that bringeth forth his fruit in his season; his leaf also shall not wither; and whatsoever he doeth shall prosper.

Psalm 25:12-13

What man is he that feareth the Lord? him shall he teach in the way that he shall choose.

His soul shall dwell at ease; and his seed shall inherit the earth.

Psalm 37:11, 37

But the meek shall inherit the earth; and shall delight them-selves in the abundance of peace.

Mark the perfect man, and behold the upright: for the end of that man is peace.

Psalm 119:165

Great peace have they which love thy law: and nothing shall offend them.

Isaiah 26:3, 12

Thou will keep him in perfect peace, whose mind is stayed on thee: because he trusteth in thee.

Lord, thou wilt ordain peace for us: for thou also hast wrought all our works in us.

Isaiah 55:12

For ye shall go out with joy, and be led forth with peace: the mountains and the hills shall break forth before you into singing, and an the trees of the field shall clap their hands.

John 14:27

Peace I leave with you, my peace I give unto you: not as the world giveth, give I unto you. Let not your heart be troubled, nei-ther let it be afraid.

Romans 14:17-19

For the kingdom of God is not meat and drink; but right-eousness, and peace, and joy in the Holy Ghost.

For he that in these things serveth Christ is acceptable to God, and approved of men.

Let us therefore follow after the things which make for peace, and things wherewith one may edify another.

Romans 15:13

Now the God of hope fill you with all joy and peace in believing that ye may abound in hope, through the power of the Holy Ghost.

2 Corinthians 13:11

Finally, brethren, farewell. Be perfect, be of good comfort, be of one mind, live in peace; and the God of love and peace shall be with you.

Philippians 4:6-7

Be careful for nothing; but in every thing by prayer and supplication with thanksgiving let your requests be made known unto God.

And the peace of God, which passeth all understanding, shall keep your hearts and minds through Christ Jesus.

When People Slander You

Job 4:19-21

How much less in them that dwell in houses of clay, whose foundation is in the dust, which are crushed before the moth?

They are destroyed from morning to evening: they perish for ever without any regarding it.

Doth not their excellency which is in them go away? they die, even without wisdom.

Job 42:7-10

And it was so, that after the Lord had spoken these words unto Job, the Lord said to Eliphaz the Temanite, My wrath is kindled against thee, and against thy two friends: for ye have not spoken of me the thing that is right, as my servant Job hath.

Therefore take unto you now seven bullocks and seven rams, and go to my servant Job, and offer up for yourselves a burnt offering; and my servant Job shall pray for you: for him will I accept: lest I deal with you after your folly, in that ye have not spoken of me the thing which is right, like my servant Job.

So Eliphaz the Temanite and Bildad the Shubite and Zophar the Naamathite went, and did according as the Lord commanded them: the Lord also accepted Job.

And the Lord turned the captivity of Job, when he prayed for his friends: also the Lord gave Job twice as much as he had before.

Psalm 31:20-24

Thou shalt hide them in the secret of thy presence from the pride of man: thou shalt keep them secretly in a pavilion from the strife of tongues.

Blessed be the Lord: for he hath shewed me his marvellous kindness in a strong city.

For I said in my haste, I am cut off from before thine eyes: nevertheless thou heardest the voice of my supplications when I cried unto thee.

O love the Lord, all ye his saints: for the Lord preserveth the faithful, and plentifully rewardeth the proud doer.

Be of good courage, and he shall strengthen your heart, an ye that hope in the Lord.

Psalm 57:3-11

He shall send from heaven, and save me from the reproach of him that would swallow me up. Selah. God shall send forth his mercy and his truth.

My soul is among lions: and I lie even among them that are set on fire, even the sons of men, whose teeth are spears and arrows, and their tongue a sharp sword.

Be thou exalted, O God, above the heavens; let thy glory be above all the earth.

They have prepared a net for my steps; my soul is bowed down: they have digged a pit before me, into the midst whereof they are fallen themselves. Selah.

My heart is fixed, O God, my heart is fixed: I will sing and give praise.

Awake up, my glory; awake, psaltery and harp: I myself will awake early.

I will praise thee, O Lord, among the people: I will sing unto thee among the nations.

For thy mercy is great unto the heavens, and thy truth unto the clouds.

Be thou exalted, O God, above the heavens: let thy glory be above all the earth.

Proverbs 6:16-21

These six things doth the Lord hate: yea, seven are an abomination unto him:

A proud look, a lying tongue, and hands that shed innocent blood,

An heart that deviseth wicked imaginations, feet that be swift in running to mischief,

A false witness that speaketh lies, and he that soweth discord among brethren.

My son, keep thy father's commandment, and forsake not the law of thy mother:

Bind the continually upon thine heart, and tie them about thy neck.

Matthew 5:10-12

Blessed are they which are persecuted for righteousness' sake: for theirs is the kingdom of heaven.

Blessed are ye, when men shall revile you, and persecute you, and shall say all manner of evil against you falsely, for my sake.

Rejoice, and be exceeding glad: for great is your reward in heaven: for so persecuted they the prophets which were before you.

Luke 1:70-79

As he spake by the mouth of his holy prophets, which have been since the world began:

That we should be saved from our enemies, and from the hand of all that hate us;

To perform the mercy promised to our fathers, and to remember his holy covenant;

The oath which he sware to our father Abraham,

That he would grant unto us, that we being delivered out of the hand of our enemies might serve him without fear,

In holiness and righteousness before him, all the days of our life.

And thou, child, shalt be called the prophet of the Highest for thou shalt go before the face of the Lord to prepare his ways.

To give knowledge of salvation unto his people by the remissions of their sin,

Through the tender mercy of our God; whereby the dayspring from on high hath visited us,

To give light to them that sit in darkness and in the shadow of death, to guide our feet into the way of peace.

1 Peter 4:12-14

Beloved, think it not strange concerning the fiery trial which is to try you, as though some strange thing happened unto you:

But rejoice, inasmuch as ye are partakers of Christ's sufferings; that, when his glory shall be revealed, ye may be glad also with exceeding joy.

If ye be reproached for the name of Christ, happy are ye; for the spirit of glory and of God resteth upon you: on their part he is evil spoken of, but on your part he is glorified.

When You Are in Need of Reassurance That Your Resources Are Sufficient

Psalm 63:5-6

My soul shall be satisfied as with marrow and fatness; and my mouth shall praise thee with joyful lips:

When I remember thee upon my bed, and meditate on thee in the night watches.

Psalm 103:2-4

Bless the Lord, O my soul, and forget not all his benefits:

Who forgiveth all thine iniquities; who healeth all thy disease;

Who redeemeth thy life from destruction; who crowneth thee with lovingkindness and tender mercies;

Isaiah 58:10-11

And if thou draw out thy soul to the hungry, and satisfy the afflicted soul; then shall thy light rise in obscurity, and thy darkness be as the noon day:

And the Lord shall guide thee continually, and satisfy thy soul in drought, and make fat thy bones: and thou shalt be like a watered garden, and like a spring of water, whose waters fail not.

Joel 2:26

And ye shall eat in plenty, and be satisfied, and praise the name of the Lord your God, that hath dealt wondrously with you: and my people shall never be ashamed.

Matthew 21:22

And all things, whatsoever ye shall ask in prayer, believing, ye shall receive.

Mark 11:24

Therefore I say unto you, What things soever ye desire, when ye pray, believe that ye receive them, and ye shall have them.

John 4:13-14

Jesus answered and said unto her, Whosoever drinketh of this water shall thirst again:

But whosoever drinketh of the water that I shall give him shall never thirst; but the water that I shall give him shall be in a well of water springing up into everlasting life.

John 16:23-24

And in that day ye shall ask me nothing. Verily, verily, I say unto you, Whatsoever ye shall ask the Father in my name, he will give it you.

Hitherto have ye asked nothing in my name: ask, and ye shall receive, that your joy may be full.

Romans 8:32

He that spared not his own Son, but delivered him up for us all, how shall he not with him also freely give us an things?

2 Corinthians 9:8

And God is able to make all grace abound toward you; that ye, always having all sufficiency in all things, may abound to every good work:

2 Corinthians 12:9

And he said unto me, My grace is sufficient for thee: for my strength is made perfect in weakness. Most gladly therefore will I rather glory in my infirmities, that the power of Christ may rest upon me.

Ephesians 1:3, 19

Blessed be the God and Father of our Lord Jesus Christ, who hath blessed us with all spiritual blessings in heavenly places in Christ:

And what is the exceeding greatness of his power to us-ward who believe, according to the working of his mighty power,

Philippians 4:13, 19

I can do all things through Christ which strengtheneth me.

But my God shall supply all your need according to his riches in glory by Christ Jesus.

2 Peter 1:3-4

According as his divine power hath given unto us all things that pertain unto life and godliness, through the knowledge of him that hath called us to glory and virtue:

Whereby are given unto us exceeding great and precious promises: that by these ye might be partakers of the divine nature, having escaped the corruption that is in the world through lust.

NOTES

NOTES

_____

_____

_____

_____

_____

_____

_____

_____

_____

_____

_____

_____

NOTES

_____

_____

_____

_____

_____

_____

_____

_____

_____

_____

_____

_____